PATHWAY THROUGH GRIEF

Pathway Through Grief

Edited by
JEAN WATSON

CHRISTINA PRESS
CROWBOROUGH, EAST SUSSEX

First published in Great Britain 1997

British Library Cataloguing Data
A catalogue record for this book is available
from The British Library.

ISBN 1 901387 05 4

Designed and produced by Bookprint Creative Services
P.O. Box 827, BN21 3YJ, England for
CHRISTINA PRESS LTD
Highland House, Aviemore Road
Crowborough, East Sussex, TN6 1QX.
Printed in Great Britain.

In memory
of our loved ones,
with love and thanks
to our families and friends

Contents

Foreword

Writing this book has proved painfully therapeutic for the ten of us who have shared our experiences of losing a much-loved marriage partner. For some, bereavement came with total suddenness, for others it followed illness. Some of us were young, others older. Eight of us are women, two are men. We write from between one and twelve years after our bereavement. You will find that we differ from one another as individuals and in the pattern of our lives. Not surprisingly, therefore, no two stories are alike.

In view of our common theme and shared faith, it's no surprise that our stories also echo one another. Various thoughts, ideas and images keep recurring as we write about our feelings and the adjustments we had to make, try to relate our faith to our anguish, and reflect on the part played by other people and the outside world on our pathway through loss.

We lovingly offer this book to all those who mourn, hoping that they will find comfort and reassurance in being able to identify with at least some of what we have written, while feeling free to be themselves and do things in their own unique ways. We also hope that others, particularly those involved through ties of friendship or kinship with bereaved people, might glean some useful insights from reading our honest, personal stories.

Jean Watson

Jean's Story

Jean Watson lives in Sevenoaks, Kent. She is the mother of three married children, Malcolm, Rachel and Esther, and has written devotional and children's books. She has worked as a volunteer with Victim Support and is currently on the committee of a local counselling service.

Jean's story was begun a year and four months after the death of her husband Mike.

Mike was lying on a hospital trolley in the next room with his face uncovered. Esther sobbed out something like, 'Dad, Oh my Dad,' and ran to hide behind a screen. One of the others went to comfort her. It hurt me later that it wasn't me, but at the time I was bending down to kiss my husband's broad forehead again and again, crying and calling out, 'Oh Mike, Oh my darling, my sweetheart.' . . . It was as I kissed him that I knew he had gone from me physically: we had been amputated from one another and, in my case, without an anaesthetic.

Jean's story

I wake each morning to the nightmare of your absence. Oh Mike, Mike, Mike, Mike. . . .

Those were the first words I wrote after my husband's unexpected and untimely death in September 1995. Mike had been a fit, athletic man looking years younger than fifty-nine. But what I and a few close friends knew was that he had been seeing specialists about the possibility of having surgery to relieve the appalling back and leg pain from which he had been suffering with tremendous courage for many years. The same few people also knew that ten years earlier he had gone into hospital for an operation – only to be sent home, feeling deeply let down. On that occasion, the consultant had changed his mind about operating: in his opinion, surgery might not solve Mike's problem; it could even make it worse. But ten years on, we hoped that the medical profession would have more to offer. And at first we were not disappointed.

Shortly before his sixtieth birthday, for which I was planning a surprise party, Mike saw a neurosurgeon who was confident that he could help him. I remember him ringing me from the hospital to give me the good news.

'Such a nice chap,' he said, referring to the neurosurgeon, and then added, with a touching note of relief in his voice, 'He understood. He knew exactly where the pain was and what it was like.' And I thought, not for the first time, of how isolated my husband must often have felt – enduring something which few people knew about or understood at all, and for which up till then no one had been able to offer any help. If anyone deserved to be given relief at long last, he did. He went on to say that the surgeon had assured him that he had successfully performed many operations for people with his problem, and was confident that he would be mobile in time for our son's wedding in two months and swimming again within a month.

It was in that context that Mike took the decision to have the surgery. The operation took place on 30th September. To us, the family, waiting on the end of the telephone, it seemed to be going on for a long time, which was very worrying, but when the anaesthetist kindly telephoned to say that everything had gone well, we felt reassured. She told my daughter Esther, who took the call, that it'd be fine for us to come up by train and see Mike in recovery – briefly, of course.

So Esther and I took the evening train to London. At the hospital I couldn't understand, didn't want to understand, why we weren't immediately told that Mike was all right and taken to see him. The nurse to whom we spoke went into a ward and spoke to a colleague, who pulled a face. My anxiety level instantly soared but I tried to tell myself that I was letting my over-active imagination run away with me.

'I just want to know that he's all right,' I said to the nurse.

She answered evasively, 'I'm afraid I've only just come on duty, but someone will be with you soon.'

She ushered us into a little room and asked us to wait. I was glad of Esther's companionship and calming presence.

After what seemed like a very long time but was probably only moments, the door opened and in they came, unsmiling and in their operating gear: a surgeon, anaesthetist and nurse. That was when the nightmare really began.

I remember the surgeon saying something like: 'I'm afraid things didn't go as we'd expected.' And then I cried out, 'You're not trying to tell me he's dead. You can't be telling me that.'

'I'm afraid I am,' he said.

'Oh no, Oh no, Oh no, you can't be saying that, you can't be. . . .' I moaned and sobbed out the words, or something like them, over and over again. This wasn't happening. Or if it was it would kill me or render me insensible. Anything would be preferable to what we were hearing and feeling.

But the surgeon's grave face and quiet voice were real enough and he was telling us that all had been going well when suddenly, after the anaesthetist's reassuring phone call to us, Mike's heart had stopped. There had been no warning and no one understood why it had happened. Resuscitation had been immediately applied – to no avail. There would have to be an inquest. He was very, very sorry, he said, and looked it. So did the nurse and anaesthetist.

My daughter and I clung to one another wordlessly. I felt dreadfully ill and faint and thought, as far as it was possible to think at all within the stupefying fog of anguish that was surrounding us, how impossibly ghastly it would be for my family if I had a heart attack and died then and there. I was sure it could happen at any moment and – but for my family – perhaps even wanted it to. Dully I asked whether I should take a tranquilliser. The anaesthetist took my pulse and someone fetched me a glass of water and I took a pill.

I don't know how long we sat there, stunned, silent, beyond tears. Then, as if by mutual consent, we found ourselves getting up to hug one another. How hard it must have been for the three professionals to have experienced what they just had and then been faced with telling us about it. That thought did somehow register, but for the most part I was isolated within my own individualised shock and pain.

Some time later I asked, 'Can I see him?'

Mike was lying on a hospital trolley in the next room with his face uncovered. Esther sobbed out something like, 'Dad, Oh my Dad,' and ran to hide behind a screen. One of the others went to comfort her. It hurt me later that it wasn't me, but at the time, I was bending down to kiss my husband's broad forehead again and again, crying, and calling out, 'Oh Mike, Oh my darling, my sweetheart.' But I knew he was not inside the body which I loved so deeply and intimately. For his face was cold and hard and unresponsive – and he was never ever that to me. His complete acceptance of me was what had helped me, over the years of our marriage, to drop my defences and feel that I and what I had to offer were precious and valuable.

It was as I kissed him that I knew that he had gone from me physically: we had been amputated from one another and, in my case, without an anaesthetic.

We returned to the room and sat down in an unimaginable state. I think it was then that I tried to tell the surgeon and the other two that Mike was an exceptional person – a lovely human being. They assured me that they had realised this even in the few brief contacts they had had with him.

They arranged for a taxi to take us home. I sat leaning my head against Esther as we drove through the night. We hardly spoke at all. Once I said, 'It's not a nightmare, it's really happened, hasn't it?' And she said with infinite sadness, 'Yes, Mum.'

But despite my question and her response, the sense of nightmarish unreality persisted. Shock, numbness and sheer incredulity kept coming and going as reality kicked in at different levels and in different ways.

One unforgettable day I had been writing on my word-processor one of the innumerable letters I was having to type, photocopy and send out at that time. Suddenly my automatic pilot mode failed and I found myself staring aghast at the sentence I had just written, as if registering its meaning for the first time. It was about Mike and ended with the words 'he died'.

I happened to be alone – mercifully, a rare occurrence in those early days – so no one saw or heard me as I proceeded, rather uncharacteristically, to stumble blindly round the house sobbing and crying out, at first in shocked disbelief and finally in appalled acceptance, 'He died, he died, he died, he died. . . .'

Over and over again in the months that followed, I'd find myself thinking or saying out loud, 'He couldn't have died – but he has. It couldn't have happened – but it did. I can't believe it – but I must.'

When on my own, especially at night in my king-size bed, I would find myself pleading with the darkness or the empty air, 'Give me five minutes, please just five minutes, or even a few seconds, so that I can hug him and kiss him and say goodbye. He can't have gone, just like that!'

All kinds of emotions buffeted me. I felt sheer anguish at the loss of Mike. My whole being ached to see him, hear him, feel him, dream of him. I guess what I was experiencing was the emotional equivalent of being physically amputated or of having had several layers of skin torn off. I felt raw and sore, wounded and weak, insecure and vulnerable. And I felt shocked and stunned, drained and exhausted, lightweight and lost, dull and disorientated, empty and purposeless, lonely and alone, sick with dread and terribly taut. Also, whenever I tried to relate to God or to begin to make any kind of sense of what had happened, I felt fear, pain and confusion.

I knew I was supposed to feel anger but simply had no energy for it and no desire whatever to cause hurt to anyone else through it. Besides, with whom was I supposed to be angry? It had been no one's fault that Mike had died and my contacts with the surgeon and anaesthetist had convinced me that they were good, honourable people who were devastated by what had happened. Was it God's fault then? I couldn't go into all that just then – not when I needed to cry desperately to him for help. The time for such questions would come, but not when life was a matter of getting from one moment to the next.

Different emotions would build up to a peak and need to be given some outlet or form of expression. Tearful, audible crying, I found could bring release, followed often by exhaustion. But there was a kind of dry, silent crying that sometimes came first and was incredibly painful. I remember in the early weeks when people were nearly always around, I often had to retreat to the nearest bathroom and lock myself in so as to be able to get through the pain barrier somehow and rejoin 'the party' – where I often felt like a spectre at the feast, while at the same time appreciating all the invitations to go out and do things with people and in fact accepting most of them.

The presence, hospitality, thoughtfulness and practical assistance of sensitive, understanding friends helped enormously as one by one each first anniversary was somehow managed. I was especially grateful to the few with whom I felt able to share some of the really deep moments of grief, and who kept speaking of Mike and allowing me to do the same. I wanted to talk about him a great deal but came to accept that some people misunderstood or couldn't cope with that. I also wanted to 'talk' to him – which I did, out loud or in my heart, when in the house on my own. I seemed to need to keep saying his name over and over again, telling him how much I loved him, weeping that I had not voiced this to him more often, comforting myself that he had indeed known this and understood the intensity beneath my reticence and privacy.

Over the first year, a good many of my responses were desperate, instinctive survival-mode ones. I avoided, for example, books, radio or television programmes which might distress or even surprise me in any way. Hence it was back to Jane Austen and other known, safe books, films and videos. Poor concentration made any sort of viewing, listening or reading very patchy but gentle, happy stories, usually set in the past, provided some distraction, comfort and sense of security.

By contrast, the contemporary world appeared to be full of nothing but death and dying, pain and suffering. Either that or suffocating triviality. As far as I was concerned, the radio and television news presenters might just as well have said, 'Here is the nine o'clock – or whatever time it happened to be – distillation of global gloom and doom'; and the presenters of many of the so-called entertainment programmes: 'Welcome to half an hour of utterly pointless inanity.' How could anyone cope with constant, regular doses of the one or be bothered with the other? I certainly couldn't.

In life, however, tragedy and trauma kept intruding. Awful things seemed to keep happening to people I admired and cared for. Six months after Mike's death, my mother died and our family was again faced with getting hold of a death certificate, contacting large numbers of people and arranging a funeral and two services. But in other ways things were very different, the grieving and questions having been triggered off years earlier when her life and personality had begun to deteriorate as the result of a stroke. More strokes and more deterioration had followed. After her death, we, particularly my father who had been in a kind of painful limbo for many years, could start to grieve properly. But it was a very hard time all the same, made harder by the context.

By now I was well into writing what I came to call my 'letters to heaven'. In a notebook or on my word-processor I wrote letters to Mike about what I would have been sharing with him had he not died and letters to God about what I needed to rethink in the light of what had happened. When Mum died, I wrote about that too – and about the questions raised by her ghastly prolonged illness.

I also wrote about the good things that happened. The one that stands out above everything else in that first year took place only weeks after Mike's thanksgiving service. This was our son's wedding which went ahead as planned and as his father would have wished. Kate and all the other members of Malcolm's new family were absolutely wonderful and, despite all the pain, the wedding was a lovely, joyful occasion. Indeed, perhaps *because* of all the pain it was extra special.

The fact that Mike and I had met with Malcolm's future in-laws at all was rather amazing. We had turned down another invitation in order to have a weekend with them, with no inkling that this would prove to be the one and only time all four of us would meet. Our stay at their home, and the way we all got on so well, is now among my most treasured memories; as is the mini-holiday Mike took me on afterwards. I had forgotten to pack a nightie and, feeling almost like a honeymoon couple again, we had gone to a chain store and bought a glamorous garment – which now reminds me very poignantly of that time of fun and closeness.

Then there are the photographs which might so easily never have been taken. Not long before their wedding, when Kate and Malcolm were with us for the weekend, Mike suddenly suggested a photo session. So we went into the garden and snapped away for a few moments. The resulting pictures of Mike with his son and future daughter-in-law are priceless. Among these are some taken by me, of Mike with one arm around Kate's shoulders and the other around Malcolm's; they, along with some casual, happy shots, taken by Kate or Malcolm, of Mike and me together, evoke thoughts too deep for words.

Some time after the wedding, I wrote in a 'letter to God':

A funeral and a wedding – so close together! How did we survive all that joy and pain, all that hard work and socialising? I can only believe you helped us – through a whole host of people reflecting your compassion. But now I am down in the depths, with the awful inquest ahead and then Christmas. I feel as if I cannot bear it. And what am I to do about these fears? When I leave the house I think, 'What if I don't return?' When I go to bed: 'Will I die tonight?' I am obsessed with getting my affairs and the house and garden in order. I exhaust myself and bring on panic attacks as I rush about. I don't want to leave a mess for my loved ones, or anything that would cause unnecessary hurt or misunderstanding. I was in a fever until my will was properly completed and filed.

Dreadful disaster scenarios keep playing and replaying before my mind's eye. This, I suppose, is the downside of having a vivid imagination. I have read so often that perfect love casts out fear. Well, I reckon being married to Mike for thirty-two years gave me much more than a pale reflection of that perfect love. But to whom can I turn now? I keep turning to you and experiencing not love but pain. Because the time-long dilemma of evil and suffering in a world which, so we read, you made, love and are in charge of, has become a totally non-academic and utterly personal question which is worrying away at me constantly. But it's at an undercurrent level. Some time I shall have to try to confront some of those thoughts and feelings openly, by writing them down, perhaps. For the moment, just help me, somehow, moment by moment, to keep going.

More than anything else, it was love that kept me going. I think it must have been through prayer – other people's perhaps rather than my own few, faint and feeble efforts – that I was able to resist, by and large, the temptation to withdraw from love which, after all, inflicts as well as heals life's deepest wounds.

Even in the very early days after Mike's death, I had at times an overwhelming sense of needing and wanting to love and be loved. I felt incredible love for Mike, and a deep sense of his love for me. I knew I had been cut off from his love in a physical sense – and this brought indescribable pangs of anguish and an aching emptiness. But I still sensed his love reaching me through our children above all; but also through memories, and through our home in which all sorts of objects in every room spoke of his care and hard work for me and the family.

As well as feeling love for Mike and love from him, I felt loved by and love for my immediate family as perhaps never before. The closeness brought about by such shared love and grief is indescribably precious.

I shall never forget gathering in a bedroom to read Mike's will. It was hand-written on a small sheet of letter-paper and signed by a friend's cleaning lady – all perfectly in order and legal but so typical of Mike's low-key, unstuffy approach to life and people. On this occasion as on others, we wept together certainly but we also laughed as we shared happy, humorous memories of an unforgettable and unique husband and father.

My amazing family had borne the brunt of communicating our shocking news to our relations, friends and neighbours, as well as to the people Mike had worked with and those he had swum with early every morning at our local pool. The response of all these people added to our sense of being loved and cared for. They telephoned, sent flowers, cards and letters, brought round or invited us out to meals, gave us lifts and practical support in so many ways. The letters and cards were full of warm tributes to Mike: he would have been amazed and embarrassed by it all, but we loved hearing about how much his unselfishness and beaming smile, his sense of humour and warmth, his common sense and reliability had been noticed and appreciated. People also wrote to assure us of their love and prayers for us and to offer practical help. I put the cards and letters into four large files which are still with me. Something that touched me very deeply was the visit of my sister and brother-in-law from New Zealand. They stayed for six weeks and helped me and the rest of my grief-stricken family in countless ways.

Only, I believe, because of all that loving support and prayer, was I able to keep going and do what I felt compelled to do: take myself off to my study to write, photocopy and send out hundreds of letters and draft out the funeral and thanksgiving services. My family were with me day and night in the early days, supported by special friends. Although he and Kate had their wedding to prepare for, Malcolm fielded a great deal of the legal and business side of things and they both travelled down from Ipswich regularly. Another huge blessing to me was the fact that Esther, married to Tony, and Rachel, married to Wayne, lived locally and they came round a great deal and helped in countless ways emotionally and practically. Together we managed to get through all the business connected with death and a funeral – such as liaising with the undertaker, florist, vicar, preacher, organist, printer, cemetery officer, caterers, solicitor.

Because of love, we got through it all, and occasions which could have been sheer torture had their amazing, even humorous, aspects or moments. An extract from a 'letter to Mike' illustrates this:

Yes, that morning burial service was very, very special, attended by family and a few special friends. And amazingly, there was laughter as well as pain. While we were waiting for the service to start, the friend who had come to play the organ and who had arrived predictably at the very last minute or even a little late, came across to give me a hug and to whisper with fond amusement that as you, dearest Mike, had always chuckled and teased her about her unpunctuality, it wouldn't really have done for her to have arrived early – or words to that effect. This reminder of your sense of fun struck just the right note for me. And a bit later, on glancing down at my clothes and realising that my neckline had plunged somewhat, I adjusted it with a grin, commenting *sotte voce* to Esther sitting beside me on the impropriety of showing cleavage on such an occasion. Quick as a flash, she whispered back, 'Mum,

Dad would have loved it!' And we exchanged smiles –
because she was right – you would have! You were always so
normal about such things – it is one of the things I love you for
(I am using the present advisedly because I do still love you in
all the ways I still can).

The thanksgiving service in the afternoon was not just
attended by family, close friends and neighbours, but also
by people in other areas of Mike's life. There was even a
representative from the army – Mike having done three
years national service with them after leaving school. Very
touchingly, the swimmers came to the service too and also
sent a stunning wreath which spelt out 6.30 – the time of
their early morning swim. A large contingent of Mike's
work colleagues and customers drove down from the
Midlands for the occasion; he had numbered many of them
among his friends and the feeling was obviously mutual.
The firm could not have been more helpful to me and the
family then and later.

I found the services, including the talks by our vicar
friend Roger Curl, very moving and inspiring, and many
others seemed to feel the same way. In both of them, I and
the family wanted to highlight Mike as a unique human
being. At the thanksgiving service particularly, many tributes, taken from letters and cards received, were read out
by friends; another friend read out both my tribute and the
one from Malcolm, Rachel and Esther. I was and am convinced that paying honest tribute to people does not
detract from God's glory. On the contrary, if we had not
been able to say good things about someone whom God
had been in charge of 'shaping up' for more than fifty
years, we would surely, by implication, be dishonouring
him! Tributes to Mike were also tributes to the God who
had made and lived in him and been reflected in so many
ways through his character and relationships, life and
work.

Mike was indeed a man truly loved and people contributed generously to a memorial fund in his memory which was given, fittingly we felt, to Tear Fund work in and around Mussoorie Hospital, where he was born. India was the country where he spent much of his early childhood.

After all the busyness and comings and goings, the loneliness and pain bit deeply again. One of my responses was to keep busy. In fact, I went into a fever of activity. For one thing, I learnt to shop. I use the 'L' word advisedly because Mike ·had been brilliant at and done almost all the shopping, though I had sometimes tagged along as an inexperienced helper. It became a not inaccurate family joke that while I stood and considered which sort of apple to buy, Mike would whizz round and do a complete shop and then return to help me make up my mind. And – as I now remember with amazed gratitude – he was always so good-humoured about this, as about all my foibles and inadequacies.

Anyway, shopping would now be my province so I had to learn how to do it. Esther and Rachel, who are far more street-wise than I am, took turns in taking me to the supermarket and elsewhere and teaching me various new skills. They were wonderful. But in those early days I would wander up and down the aisles in a daze, wondering bemusedly, 'Why am I here? What am I doing? Where's Mike? What's this all about?'

The same applied to other activities, but I busied myself with them too: cleaning, clearing, reordering, decorating. I also, very quickly, continued to take in lodgers, as Mike and I had done together before. This involved flexibility and effort but worked out well because I didn't like rattling around alone in rather a big house and, as a bonus, I liked and got on with everyone who came and stayed.

Much later I tried to work out why I had apparently changed my basic orientation from contemplation to activism. I decided that it had something to do with trying to reduce my sense of panic and vulnerability, by gaining some sort of control over at least some areas of my life. As I looked round the house and garden and realised that it was all my responsibility now, I felt utterly overwhelmed. Mike had carried the heavy end of home management, generously leaving me free to do the things he thought I was good at – writing, seeing people, doing voluntary work, cooking. Somehow I had to try to make things more manageable; to exert control where I still could. So, often in a dazed, frenzied way, I focused on Mike's files and finances and other things in the house or garden, with a view to simplifying or organising everything as well as I could.

But there was more to my motivation than that, I believe. Obsessed as I was at the time with the idea of sudden death, I felt compelled by loving duty to try to leave everything as shipshape as possible for my loved ones to deal with after I had gone. Also, the frenetic busyness provided a welcome, if temporary and partial, distraction from the turbulence and pain within while, at the same time, helping me to feel purposeful and contributing to a sense of continuity, both of which were crucial to me. I had lost Mike's physical presence, and I could do nothing whatever about that devastating fact. But what I had not lost of him I was determined to retain and make the most of.

For one thing, I still had memories to be kept alive in every way possible: through continuing my 'letters' and through persisting in 'talking' to him when I was alone in the house and bringing him into conversations when I was with others. For another, I still had Mike's things in the house. I know many people put away, or get charity workers to take away, their loved one's things. But I wanted family members to have what they wished and to leave the rest, after some necessary sorting and sifting, more or less in place: not as a shrine to Mike but simply to give myself more time. True, I often found myself gasping, doubling up and weeping, at the sight of something of Mike's which evoked a memory and which at the same time brought home to me my loss. But it was the option I preferred.

Sometimes I deliberately put his possessions in places where I would have to see them regularly. This seemed better, and a quicker way of exorcising the pain, than coming across them occasionally and unexpectedly on opening a drawer or box, for instance. Mike's fairly new walking boots came in for this treatment. Finding them in the garage one day caused me really piercing anguish, as I was reminded of an activity which my husband loved and which he had been hoping the operation would finally allow him to do with enjoyment again. So I put them in his study which I had made into mine, where I saw them often, before giving them with pain but much love to Malcolm.

Something else I did was to go through all the family photographs – hundreds of them. And I bought countless albums and picture frames and arranged photos of Mike alone or with his family and friends in them. Of course, I often wept as I did all this, mostly on my own. But I felt it was worth it in order to be surrounded by, or have close at hand, reminders of special holidays and good times; of, in particular, Mike's physical presence and our life together.

Two things which could have helped me to feel less disconnected and more in control and purposeful, but didn't at first, were reading and writing. I kept about a dozen tried and trusted books on my bed, beside my pillow, where I could easily reach them when I woke from one form of nightmare to another and needed words of love, comfort and reassurance. But dipping into a few 'safe' books now and then was a far cry from reading avidly and being able to lose myself in all kinds of stories as I had done before. Fortunately, spoken word cassettes helped to fill some of the vacuum as far as reading was concerned. Particularly at night when I was trying to get to sleep or had woken at some unearthly hour and felt alone and sad and afraid, I would switch on a familiar story and find a measure of distraction and relief.

As for writing, I still had to do it, of course. There were hundreds of letters to deal with, for the post was – and continued for some time to be – very heavy. In addition to keeping in touch with countless friends and well-wishers, I had to deal with business and advertising mail of which there was plenty. Conscientiously and painfully, week after week, I wrote to scores of people, firms and organisations telling them what had happened and asking that they should cross us off all their mailing lists. Some complied; others did not. In the end, but only after all else had failed, I resorted, sadly, to writing: 'Deceased – return to sender'. As well as dealing with all this, I was also updating my letters to heaven, but whether I would ever write books for others again, I did not really know.

Mercifully, during the second year, my ability to concentrate is returning and reading and writing, as I used to experience them, are coming into their own again. I find joy in them once more, but also, inevitably, pain, even when I am not writing or reading specifically around life's darker themes. For I will never again be able to share ideas with Mike; or to read aloud something which I have enjoyed and want him to enjoy too, or something on which I need his comments and reactions. As a writer I was used to being solitary, but it was solitariness in the context of Mike's character and presence and of our life together. Now that he is no longer around – in his study close to mine, downstairs reading, or out visiting customers but soon to return – these pursuits can feel not just solitary but also lonely and pointless.

Near the first anniversary of Mike's death, I heard from the surgeon and anaesthetist to whom I had written after the inquest. He said that he was still performing the same operation and still had no idea why things had gone so tragically wrong when he had been operating on Mike; and she wrote a long and very moving letter of sympathy and also sent a basket of exquisite blooms. I was deeply touched by this continuing contact as I was by friends and family who went on making space for me in their busy lives.

Little by little, I am getting through the pain barrier more easily and becoming, I hope, more courageous; more prepared to face, now and then, what might disturb or surprise me; more willing to take the risk of writing again with commitment and honesty. Mike took on and sacrificed so much in order to free me to write, and encouraged me so often, that it would be sad indeed if I wasn't able to continue. Especially now that I have even more to say in certain areas. (Would that I didn't – at the price!)

One of these areas is love. I've said a lot about my need and experience of human love. But what of God's love? Direct experiences of this, or even of his 'speaking' through the Bible seemed rare at first. But I gradually came to see that he was indeed loving me – chiefly through people, but also through his creation and his sustaining of the world from which I was benefiting in ways which I had previously taken somewhat for granted. I began to see God's love, for example, behind the quiet, ordinary structures of everyday life: 'the trivial round, the common task'; undemanding social interaction. In time and with support I was able to manage such things again and they – as it were – bought me time and helped me from moment to moment while the long, slow process of grieving went on inside.

God's love reached me too, through the beauty of the world. Mike, more than anyone, had taught me to notice and enjoy the living world and creatures, starting in our own back garden, which to him was a constant source of interest and delight. I know many bereaved people resent the uncaring beauty of nature and the relentless regularity of the seasons. But I kept trying to see and enjoy everything as he would have done. This was poignant and painful certainly but also healing and comforting. The autumn after Mike's death was as stunningly colourful as any I can ever remember and my delight in it brighter because I had known Mike, but at the same time crisscrossed by deeper shadows because of his loss.

As with love and beauty, reality too had its shadowed side but here again I was helped to remain open and committed to it. I remember very early on making a pact with myself that I would do my best to be honest. Truth in the inward parts had to come first, I was sure, if true healing and growth were to follow.

Being committed to reality also meant being willing, in my own time, to try to get things in perspective. And I do stress *in my own time*, because other people's advice, judgmental attitudes, suggestions as to what we 'ought' to be feeling, implications that we have passed our 'grieve by' dates are almost always counterproductive even if not actually wrong or ill-judged. It is the bereaved person who needs to come to the point of being open to perspectives which include other people's situations and suffering; and of being willing gradually to move away from the self-absorbed, over-subjective outlook of early heart-breaking grief so as to grow more clear-sighted and compassionate, become a little wiser, and develop somewhat sounder judgments.

Where does faith fit into all this? It's a question I often ponder. I took up what could be called the outward threads of my faith fairly soon after my bereavement, resuming church attendance and trying to read and pray each day as Mike and I had done together most mornings after his return, glowing and temporarily pain-free, from his early swim. But sometimes it felt like going through the motions and at other times I'd find myself crying into my Bible or notes as I sat up in bed, or fighting back tears while everyone else in church sang their heads off seemingly without a care in the world.

There was something else which made church-going difficult for me at that time. This was that while I felt I needed comfort and the reassurance of God's understanding and love, what I seemed to be hearing was about sin and my need for forgiveness. Perhaps in my vulnerability, I wasn't hearing altogether straight. Or perhaps 'conservative evangelical' churches – how I hate these labels! – do tend to focus on one aspect of the gospel.

On the plus side, attending 'my' church was familiar and safe – and this was important; the emotional openness and unpredictability of some forms of worship would have had me in total retreat from everything 'religious', I believe. Even more important, the church family were a great support and included most of my closest friends. It also included my daughter Rachel. Her presence with me week by week was very special, as was her decision to attend classes and be confirmed a year and a half after Mike's death.

Some people assume that having a Christian faith will somehow give them a short cut through their grieving process; or that they won't, or perhaps shouldn't, grieve as deeply as others. But I believe those assumptions are flawed. For the kind of grief we feel and how we deal with it have to do with three things particularly: the kind of person we are; the kind of relationship we had with the deceased; and the manner in which he or she died. Of course faith comes into each of those.

As far as I am concerned, this means that while my emotions must take their natural course, I can count on the presence, compassion and comfort of Jesus of the scars, who is God himself and the source of all true love. Active in the world now in all kinds of not necessarily obvious ways, he will ultimately wipe all tears from our eyes and welcome us to his kingdom of perfect, painless love. All this was highlighted for me one unforgettable evening.

I had gone to bed exhausted after the ordeal of the

inquest at a coroner's court in London. In this strange
place, surrounded by strangers, Malcolm had represented
me, and a medical friend had asked searching questions of
'our' surgeon and anaesthetist and of the pathologist who
had performed the autopsy. At the end of all that, a verdict
of death by misadventure had been returned, leaving no
one any wiser as to the human cause of Mike's death, but
at least there had been no negligence. The conduct of the
surgeon and anaesthetist on the stand and when we had
spoken with them afterwards had confirmed our views of
them as competent professionals and caring human
beings. But the strain on us all had been considerable and
by bedtime I was still too strung up to sleep.

Propped up against the pillows, I cried out to God for
reassurance that Mike was well and happy and with him,
and then turned to my Bible-reading notes. The heading
for the day was 'facing our pain', which sounded tough but
appropriate, while the Bible passage was about Jesus
raising someone from the dead, which could have evoked
an angry or ironic, 'I'd settle for that any day or even a bit
of sky-writing!'

Instead, I simply read the passage, and found the story
of Mary, Martha and Lazarus coming alive for me. I felt
Mary's anguished bewilderment as she said to Jesus, 'If
you had been here my brother would not have died.' And
I silently cried out, 'But you *were* there and *still* my husband
died.' Then came Jesus' reply to her and to me, 'I am the
resurrection and the life. He who believes in me will live,
even though he dies.' The response of my whole being was,
'Yes! Mike believed in him and so, though dead, now lives
with God.' A familiar, general truth became new and particular, personal and precious, to me again.

And there was more, for once again I found my whole
being responding to some other words in the story: 'Jesus
wept.' Just two words, but they brought me deep comfort
and hope. Jesus weeps with me, for my loss, just as he wept

with Mary and Martha for theirs. This I believe and hold on to for myself and others, while continuing to grapple with much that I don't understand in the whole area of prayer, suffering and God's control.

I still wake each morning to the nightmare of Mike's physical absence. But it's a nightmare I'm learning to live with, a day at a time, as, increasingly, I absorb my loss and appreciate and draw on all that I have.

Nicky's Story

Nicky Rees lives near Tunbridge Wells with her husband Gordon. She is both mother and step-mother to four teenagers, and works part-time as a production manager for a local Christian publishing company.

Nicky's story was written nearly ten years after the death of her first husband Mark.

The next two weeks passed in a kind of limbo. I couldn't eat and seemed to have an almost permanent headache. I telephoned anyone I could possibly think of who might have had news of Mark before or after his disappearance. I contacted companies in Holland who were recruiting building services engineers, to enquire whether he had taken a job with them. My in-laws and parents even hired a private detective in an effort to trace him. Everything we tried drew a blank.

Nicky's Story

On Thursday 30th September 1987, at 3.30 pm, there was a ring at the front door. I opened it to see a plain-clothes policeman standing there with a WPC by his side.

'Good afternoon, I've come to tell you that we have received some news about your husband,' he said flatly.

I leaned against the door with relief. Mark, my husband, had been missing without word for two weeks and I had been frantic with worry. They must have located him at long last. I opened the door wider and smiled broadly, 'Do come in.'

They stepped into the hall. The policeman did not return my smile, and the WPC looked uncomfortable. Then the policeman said bluntly, 'We have found your husband. But it's bad news, I'm afraid; he has taken his own life.'

I stared at him, not comprehending. Then what he had said hit me and my mouth dried up and an uncontrollable fluttering started in my stomach. I was unable to speak as the WPC took my arm and gently guided me into the sitting room and sat me down in an armchair. From upstairs came the sound of hammering as Mark's father, who had kept me company every day since his son's disappearance, continued with some carpentry work in his grandson's bedroom.

At first I felt strangely calm as the tension which had been building up inside me drained away: after all the long days of waiting I at last had some tangible news of my husband. But the shocking reality of what he had done, and the effect it would have on my life, did not make an impact for some time.

Mark and I had met on a trekking holiday in Turkey some sixteen years earlier. I had been immediately attracted by his large, expressive brown eyes which were kind and warm. As we travelled around Turkey we found ourselves spending more and more time in each other's company. He was rather reserved, so the process of getting to know one another was difficult at first, but in time conversation became easier and I began to feel very comfortable with him. We were pleased to discover that we worked in offices close by each other in London. He was finishing an apprenticeship at a firm of consulting engineers near Bond Street, and I was a private secretary at the Canadian High Commission in Grosvenor Square. We both still lived at home and commuted into work from opposite sides of the capital.

On returning home, I did not really expect to see Mark again as I was sure our stereotype holiday romance would fizzle out. However, to my surprise, he did telephone me. We soon started going out, usually meeting straight after work for a meal followed by a quiet drink, a visit to the cinema or a walk by the river. We went to rock and classical concerts whenever we could afford to, and regularly tried to see the Royal Ballet. During one memorable week, we were so successful in the allocation of tickets to see Rudolph Nuryev that we found ourselves at Covent Garden on three out of five possible nights. This, although excessive in terms of going out, was an opportunity we felt we could not afford to miss!

It transpired quite early on in our relationship that, brought up to be regular church-goers, we had also both been confirmed at fifteen. Here the similarity ended, for, as Mark confessed, he had become disillusioned with

Christianity over the intervening years whereas I had tried to build on my faith and was at that time worshipping at Sevenoaks Baptist Church and involved in its youth activities. He seemed genuinely interested in my beliefs and questioned me at length about my faith, although he did not feel he could recommit himself in any way.

I found myself gradually dropping further and further away from my church activities in Sevenoaks, partly because I usually spent most weekends with Mark and his family, and partly because he made it increasingly clear that he really was not interested in accompanying me. As time went on I realised that I had grown to love Mark very deeply and did not want to lose him, but I was confused as to how to cope with the impasse between my commitment to God and Mark's lack of interest. The only way I felt I could deal with the situation was to keep my faith to myself, so as not to disturb the peace and harmony that otherwise existed between us.

We were married in 1978 and settled in a small house in a village outside Brentwood in Essex. Mark quickly installed his large collection of bonsai trees in our tiny garden, and filled the living room with two tanks of tropical fish and a continually expanding collection of records. By now he had successfully passed his final exams and had already worked for several companies, thus gaining experience and making contacts.

Jennifer was born in 1978, a long-awaited grandchild for both families. I thought she was beautiful – very small with huge blue eyes and masses of dark hair. At first all seemed well, but as the months went by it became obvious that she was falling more and more behind in her development. She was eighteen months old before we finally obtained a diagnosis of her condition: she had severe learning difficulties and some physical disabilities. During this time Mark and I grew even closer, grieving for the child we had hoped we would have and sharing our worries for Jenny's future. We felt, and told one another, that if we could always manage to talk things through together in the way we had when coming to terms with Jenny's difficulties, we would be able to cope with anything the future might hold.

When our second child, Patrick, was born two years later, we were overjoyed that he was big and healthy. Mark was so euphoric that he went from a night in the delivery room straight into work where he broke open a bottle of malt whiskey which he had been saving for just such a celebration – I am not sure that either he or his colleagues achieved much that day!

Shortly afterwards I raised the question of when we would have the children baptised – a subject I had put to one side during the confused and stressful months following Jenny's birth. I naturally assumed that we would now have both children christened together. I was very taken aback when Mark announced that this, or even a blessing, was something he could not contemplate. I was very distressed, as my commitment to God was still firm, and I believed that the children should be baptised as babies. But Mark was adamant and stood his ground. Eventually I gave in, although I was left with a strong feeling that I had really let God, as well as Jenny and Patrick, down. So I decided that I would do my best to teach the children basic Christian beliefs as they grew up. I still used to attend church services, but as this put considerable strain on my relationship with Mark, I tended to find reasons not to go, and never provoked a row by taking the children. However I set some time aside for prayer, to ask for strength and guidance in dealing with the situation, and in particular that Mark might become less hostile towards my viewpoint and more open to allowing the children to learn about Christianity.

Over the next seven years Mark, now working for himself, continued to be moderately successful. I had tapped into a network of help and support for Jenny who had settled down at her special school in Chelmsford. When Patrick started at a small pre-prep school nearby I was able to take a part-time job at a local publishing company.

We both continued to put a lot into our work, holidays and family life, meeting and dealing with any new problem that Jenny had to face as it came along, but equally rejoicing every time she achieved a goal, however small. Mark was essentially a family man, endlessly patient and gentle with his daughter whom he adored, and extremely proud of his son who bore, and still bears, a striking resemblance to him.

It was towards the beginning of 1987 that I began to notice that Mark was becoming more and more withdrawn. There had always been an almost imperceptible part of him that I had occasionally felt unable to reach, but now, as the months went by I sensed he was trying to build a wall between us. I asked him many times whether there was anything wrong but he always assured me that all was well; that he loved me and the children and was not worried about anything; that business was continuing to go well and there was nothing he wanted to talk through with me. In the company of family and friends he was as normal and cheerful as he had always been.

I simply did not know what to do as I saw someone I loved pulling away from me; and the more I tried to get us both back on the same wavelength, the harder he resisted. I suggested gently that he should perhaps see our GP, but he refused pointblank. I felt I was being pushed aside, but hoped that in time he would eventually share whatever was troubling him. In May we went on a short holiday to southern Spain. During that week Mark became his old self and on our return home, and in the ensuing months, appeared to be much happier than he had been before.

In the middle of September 1987, Mark mentioned that he had been invited to a party to celebrate the completion of a project at London Bridge, for which he had been part of the building services design team. He warned me that as the celebrations were likely to run well into the night, he would probably stay up in London with a colleague. I agreed that this would be a sensible idea although I was a little surprised about it, since Mark had always previously made the effort to come home at night, however late. On this particular morning, however, he seemed to be in a cheerful and relaxed mood, and helped Jenny and Patrick with their breakfast, as usual, before preparing to leave for work himself.

'So it's unlikely I'll see you tonight?' I said, as he bent down to kiss me.

'Probably not,' he replied, 'but I'll give you a ring first thing in the morning just to check that you and the children are all right.'

I half-hoped that when I woke up the following morning Mark would be there beside me, but he was not. I was slightly puzzled when he didn't phone as he had promised. 'Never mind,' I thought, 'he has probably had a late night and will ring me when I get to work.' I put Jenny on her school bus, dropped Patrick at his school and went on to work.

By mid-morning when Mark had still not contacted me, I telephoned his office.

'I'm sorry, Nicky,' said the receptionist. 'Mark didn't come into work yesterday at all and he missed the party as well. We decided not to ring you because we didn't want to worry you.'

As I put the phone down I suddenly felt very frightened and unsure, and for the first time my stomach started churning. I eventually decided to telephone the police and report Mark missing. They were very reassuring and arranged to meet me at home to get a few basic details. After they had gone, I contacted my parents and in-laws, who came over immediately, and we spent the rest of the day waiting for news. When the children arrived home from school they were so delighted to see all their grandparents unexpectedly together that they did not pick up our worry and tension. Also, as it was not unusual for their father to arrive home well past their bedtime, they did not miss him.

It was mid-evening when two other policemen and a WPC turned up. This time they were extremely business-like and I was aware that while I was supplying more details, one of the policemen wandering around was showing particular interest in the back garden. Later they asked me to show them upstairs, which I did. There they searched through the bedroom cupboards and up in the loft. They then relaxed and, as they left, informed me very calmly that they were satisfied I hadn't got Mark's body hidden somewhere in the house or garden. I was speech-less – the situation was absolutely bizarre.

The following day I made some enquiries of my own and discovered that although Mark had been working solidly on one project after another, things had not been going so well financially and his company was in some debt, partic-ularly with the Inland Revenue which was pressing hard for the payment of some outstanding tax. The amount was not impossibly great but, I realised, it might explain why Mark, who had always seemed so conscientious about budgeting and saving, had become distant and distracted over the previous months. I felt a mixture of emotions: compassion for Mark who had obviously been going out of his mind with worry, but also an acute feeling of being let down because he had not confided in me. All I wanted was for him to contact me so that we could talk things through, and I was confident that, with all our family support, we could sort the mess out.

So it came as something of a shock when the police dis-covered that Mark had actually flown to Holland on the day he went missing. That much had now been ascertained, but thereafter the trail had gone cold. Given this new information, conclusive proof it would seem that Mark was still alive and had apparently chosen to disappear, the police said they would keep his name on the missing persons' file, but would not actively try to locate him. It took a huge effort for me to digest the implications of this news, while at the same time trying desperately to persuade the police that Mark's actions had been totally out of character. Despite what I said, they told me firmly there was nothing more they could do.

The next two weeks passed in a kind of limbo. I couldn't eat and seemed to have an almost permanent headache. I telephoned anyone I could possibly think of who might have had news of Mark before or after his disappearance. I contacted companies in Holland who were recruiting building services engineers, to enquire whether he had taken a job with them. My in-laws and parents even hired a private detective in an effort to trace him. Everything we tried drew a blank. My father-in-law came round every day ostensibly to build a wardrobe for Patrick. I was grateful just to have another person in the house to talk things through with and to wait with me. Of course the hardest part was explaining to the children why their father was suddenly not there any more. I told them that he had had to go away on business for a little while and that I wasn't sure exactly when he was coming back. Much to my relief, they completely accepted this explanation and continued to be immersed in their school and outside activities.

So it was with joyful anticipation that I first greeted the police when they came. But this was swiftly replaced by a numb sense of disbelief as I tried unsuccessfully to absorb the fact that Mark was not going to come home. I felt so desolate I could not even cry.

Over the next few days we managed to piece together his last movements. He had flown back from Europe, hired a car and been found dead in it from carbon monoxide poisoning the following day in a churchyard near Great Dunmow in Essex. Even in my stunned state, I registered surprise that Mark, of all people, had chosen a churchyard in which to end his days. There seemed to be a plethora of such unanswered questions or loose ends, and I had an overwhelming need to chart his last hours in an effort to gain some insight into his troubled mind. My immediate neighbours and friends took it in turns to sit with me in the evenings and listen patiently as I went over events again and again, questioning and questioning, trying to make sense of it all. My only peace came at night when I fell into a deep sleep from sheer mental exhaustion. When I woke in the morning there would be a split second of forgetfulness before my brain caught up with my body. Then reality would hit me like a wall and the whole cycle of thought would begin again.

I had been wondering about and dreading the effect of Mark's death on the children. As soon as I was able to find a quiet time with them, I told them very simply that he had died while he was away. Jenny, who was actually nine but looked at the world through the eyes of a four-year-old, immediately decided he was in heaven with our pet labrador, who had died a few months earlier, and that was that. Patrick was much quieter and did not say anything, but he sat and cried as I cuddled them both.

Fortunately the police released Mark's body quite quickly following identification by his brother and the post-mortem. Once this was done, I could see him: I knew I needed to do that before the funeral in order to say goodbye. A time was arranged and my father drove me to the undertakers and waited outside while I went in alone. As I approached the coffin and gazed at my husband's face for the first time in three weeks, I saw that indeed his body was there but he was not. On the drive home, I was full of my own confused thoughts. If he's not there, where is he? was one of the questions tormenting me.

I wanted to keep the funeral as low-key as possible. Our village rector took the service at Chelmsford crematorium and did a magnificent job, given the circumstances and the fact that Mark was not a Christian. The chapel was packed with family, friends and Mark's colleagues. I had allowed myself one tranquilliser just for this occasion, so I was able to watch the coffin in a totally detached way as the curtains closed, and to tell myself that there was just an empty shell inside it.

Immediately following the funeral I had many visitors. It is never easy to visit the bereaved, and expressing condolences to someone in my situation would have made it an even more difficult thing to do. Some of our friends were obviously struggling hard to come to terms with the news themselves, and we often comforted each other and cried together. I found the visit of one good friend especially difficult. She had been a committed Christian all her life, and as she left she promised she would be praying for me. 'You must be joking,' I thought as I closed the door behind her. 'God doesn't love me – he's allowed Mark to die.' I had not been able to pray with any conviction during the past month and simply could not see any reason to do so now.

I tried to keep busy over the next few weeks, occupying the evenings by answering every card and letter that arrived. Fortunately our solicitor, a family friend, not only guided me through all the legal formalities but bore the brunt of sorting out the financial problems as well.

I continued to sleep soundly, even through the night of the Great Storm which lifted several tiles off the roof and brought down a large tree in the garden.

The police were still trying to piece together Mark's movements over the period when he was in Europe, and their enquiries delayed the date for the inquest. I half-hoped still that they would find a note or a letter somewhere, but he had never been a great letter-writer and I thought it unlikely he would have felt like putting pen to paper, given his probable state of mind. In the meantime they returned his clothes and possessions to me in a black plastic sack, but I could not keep much because everything smelled of exhaust fumes.

I had decided to return to work in an attempt to start getting my life back into some sort of normality and to keep my thoughts occupied during the day. However, at half-term I was at home again nursing Jenny and Patrick through chicken pox, the one childhood disease I had never had. Inevitably I caught it, and was so ill that I hardly registered what would have been Mark's thirty-seventh birthday when it came. Recovery took a long time, and when I was next able to look in the mirror I wondered wryly whether Mark would have recognised me: I had lost over two-and-a-half stone, my skin was drawn and my hair uncut and lank.

If it had not been for the children I would have been glad to die as well. How was I going to manage alone for the rest of my life? Apart from bringing up two small children, how was I going to cope with the added and unknown complications of Jenny's disabilities? I experienced a mixture of emotions. Sometimes I was so angry that Mark had, as I imagined, taken the easy way out when things got tough, leaving me to pick up the pieces and bring up his children. At other times I wanted more than anything to put the clock back. I kept going over and over moments with him: trying to remember what he said; looking for clues as to what was in his mind; and above all wondering what things I didn't say but maybe should have or what signs I hadn't picked up but perhaps might have. Above all I wanted Mark back, alive, just for a few moments.

I was hardly aware of Christmas approaching, yet I was suddenly caught up in the usual round of end-of-term school nativity plays and concerts. That year Patrick's school held their carol service in Chelmsford Cathedral. I really did not feel like going but my mother insisted on taking us while my father stayed at home baby-sitting Jenny. As I sat quietly there waiting in a detached way for the service to start and trying not to see the rows of happy smiling parents with their sons sitting in between them, I found myself gazing at a side altar which had a beautifully coloured frontal on it and two glowing candles. Then my eyes came to rest on the cross and I felt myself being filled with a warmth which flowed into every part of my body. At the same time an incredible sense of peace came over me, and the oppression I had been feeling for the past four months eased. I knew then, without a doubt, that God was still with me, telling me that despite my rather jaded faith he still loved me.

It was late when we returned home and even later when Patrick eventually fell asleep, but, after my parents had left, I sat quietly and thought about God and all that he meant to me. I had not felt close to him during the past weeks because of my sense of hurt and rejection and because I had been taking a lot of my anger out on him: as I perceived it, he had allowed my husband to die – and in so very igno-minious a way. What I had not focused on were his love and compassion for me, which had been there all the time, waiting for my acceptance. As I thumbed through my Bible which I had not opened for quite a long time, I came across this verse: 'I will give you a new heart and put a new spirit in you' (Ezekiel 36:26). That night the Lord did just that for me, restoring my faith. He gave me a new heart to follow him and a new spirit with which to begin the slow process of rebuilding my life.

At the beginning of the new year, after a quiet Christmas, I decided to take Jenny and Patrick to the parish church regularly.

I was a bit wary at first: in a small village community where news travels fast, I knew it would be inevitable that many of the congregation would know our circumstances. However, everyone I met was very kind and, as time went on, I became less sensitive and started to enjoy worshipping there each Sunday, knowing this to be a way of re-establishing my relationship with God. But I never managed to feel comfortable enough for really close involvement there.

The inquest, at the beginning of February, was held at the request of the police who, failing to uncover any more evidence surrounding Mark's last days, wanted to close the case. Although there were so many unanswered questions, and still are, I felt that it would be unfair to the rest of the family to prolong things further. Mercifully the hearing was quick, with the minimum of detail and formalities.

That day marked the end of a chapter for me. The last of the red tape had been dealt with and I now had to look ahead and bring up our children as best as I could. It was Edmund Burke who said, 'The true way to mourn the dead is to take care of the living who belong to them.' Strangely enough I did not feel too daunted by this task because I now trusted that God would always give me enough strength to carry on. He had protected me during the past months in lots of ways, not only on the road when I had often driven along with tears streaming down my face, but also from having to make too many immediate decisions in my new role as single parent and sole bread-winner. I believe he gave me enough inner reserve to tackle each challenge as it came along: 'those who hope in the Lord will renew their strength' (Isaiah 40:31). I soon realised that the first time of having to deal with a new task or with a situation previously unencountered was always the hardest; and that the next time something similar cropped up I would be much better equipped to deal with it. This simple philosophy helped me to face the practicalities of running a home and a car, and of managing the finances.

Early into 1988 I received some bereavement counselling from a good friend, who was an experienced counsellor. She was able to put Mark's death into some kind of perspective and, in so doing, give me an insight into what might have been in his mind immediately prior to his suicide. The fact that Mark would not have been thinking clearly, or perceiving life realistically, would have made him see his problems as permanent and insoluble. It hurt me a lot to face the probability that he had been too self-preoccupied to think about the devastating impact his suicide would have on me, his children and the rest of his family and friends. Maybe in running away from the problem in the first place he had been hoping it would go away, and then, on his return to England, had been unable to face the fact of its being still there. I gradually came to understand and accept this interpretation of events, but it has taken me years to lose a sense of total rejection and of having failed him.

As time went on I began to get some of my old energy back and, being a natural optimist, decided that the three of us would make opportunities to do something or go somewhere new whenever we could. Activities ranged from afternoon picnics to weekend youth hostelling, and culminated in a camping holiday in France. Although there were occasions when I felt the responsibility and loneliness of my widowed status very keenly, we had some wonderful experiences and there were times when I could not understand why Mark had chosen to leave such a beautiful world behind. I tried to make each trip an adventure for us all, but I would always ask God for his guidance beforehand. Despite planning and executing these activities, that first year seemed interminable. But, gradually, the deep pain inside did begin to ease, and one day in the summer I suddenly realised that I had not consciously missed Mark for nearly half the day.

It was just before Christmas that I was unexpectedly introduced to Gordon. He was a committed Christian, with a son and daughter virtually the same age as Jenny and Patrick, and, at that time, going through the final throes of

a divorce. Though he was totally different in physical
appearance and character from Mark, from the moment we
met I felt as if I had known him all my life, and he had
exactly the same feeling about me. He lived near my
parents' home in Kent, so the M25 between Kent and Essex
was red-hot as we tried to spend as much time together as
our work and family commitments allowed. As Gordon
was actively involved in his village church, I soon got into
the habit of driving down with the children so we could
join him for the Sunday morning service. After putting
thousands of miles on our cars and making a significant
contribution in tolls to the coffers of the Dartford Tunnel,
we were married in 1991 at St Mary's Stansted, near
Sevenoaks, with special permission from the Bishop of
Rochester. Soon afterwards we made our home in
Speldhurst, a small village near Tunbridge Wells.

Over five years have passed since then. Step-parenting,
caring for four growing teenagers and dealing with an
extended-family situation have brought their own headaches, but God has continued to bless us and our marriage
in very many ways. Our village church in Speldhurst has
given us the support and fellowship of many good friends,
thus encouraging all of us to grow in faith. One of my
happiest moments has been to see Jenny and Patrick baptised at long last. It is only since coming here and being
given the opportunity to study the Bible with others and to
listen to older and wiser Christians, that I have been able
truly to forgive Mark and find peace of mind over the question that had been troubling me ever since I saw his empty
body. As Christians we are taught that suicide is a sin and
not God's will, but I console myself that only God knows
the state of someone's heart immediately before death.
Although Mark, to my knowledge, did not share my faith,
it is just possible that in that quiet churchyard, his thoughts
turned back to God even as he died.

My life has totally changed as a result of Mark's death,

but I believe God used the situation to strengthen my faith and equip me to play my part at church and in my present job in a Christian company. Jenny and Patrick are growing up, secure in a loving family atmosphere again, and they in turn have made their own commitment to God by being confirmed. I pray their faith will continue to grow. I also pray for future generations of our family: for their Christian discipleship, and that they will be protected in years to come from all the possible negative effects of these past events.

Sue's Story

Susan Bottley was a vicar's wife in Sheffield for twenty years and has three adult children, Graham, Ann and Stephen. She now works as the director of the Good News Trust – a mobile library service which has teams of workers in Great Britain and Eire.

Sue's story was written almost two years after the death of her husband David.

Everything seems more intense since David died. Somehow the deep pain and anguish is matched with an equally deep enjoyment. The beauty of the countryside near my home; flowers and shrubs; sunsets and night skies; the seaside and friendships; reading the Bible and experiencing God's presence: everything appears more vital and alive. I don't understand why this should be. . . . Perhaps our senses are dulled when life is easy or, at least, less challenging.

Sue's Story

Two landmarks today. One, my eldest son announced his engagement – long awaited by everyone. The other is starting to write this chapter. The first is about looking forward in faith and hope to a long and happy marriage; the second, about reflecting on the ending of twenty-nine years of happy marriage.

So often in life it is necessary to take the next step, and this involves facing bereavements, large or small. Leaving home to start school; changing to a larger school; moving house; leaving school for work or college; pairing up, and getting married; losing a measure of independence through marriage, mortgage, children. The losses involved in doing those things are usually accepted readily because the changes are seen as desirable. But having to give up running, squash or proper camping may not be. Certainly, losing relatives and friends, and most devastating of all, one's spouse, is in a different league altogether.

How well have I coped with this tearing apart of 'one flesh'?

I think back to 1992 when my husband David wrote this for a newsletter:

'Your kidneys will fail by the time you are sixty.' I was angry at the doctor's words. Here I was in my middle forties, an active man enjoying life to the full. Surely not!

But the doctor's words were to come true eight years ahead of time. Two months ago my kidneys were giving up and I had to begin dialysis. I have to dialyse four times a day every day for life, unless I am fortunate enough to receive a kidney transplant. This has had an immediate good effect and I find my strength returning. I am able to continue my work and enjoy walking and swimming. . . .

'Why me?' I have not found this to be a question that I ask. I have always believed and taught that sickness and death, as well as health and strength, are part of the mystery of life. Some never ail; others do. The progression of my complaint has been slow and relatively pain free. If I was in constant pain, or if my illness was sudden and terminal, my attitude might be different.

On a number of occasions I have sought prayer for God's healing. I find the account in Daniel 3:16–18 helpful in my attitude to healing. My understanding of that passage is this: whatever God chooses to do, I will still trust him. This story of these three men is a magnificent account of faith in adversity, and I find it a great comfort and inspiration. . . .

Above all I find that Jesus Christ has given me true contentment in life. The contentment that people spoke about in the early days when I was seeking Christ and then became a Christian has come true. The Lord Jesus Christ is still as exciting and fulfilling to follow in my fifties as he was in my twenties. Hallelujah, what a Saviour!

Three years later, in my Christmas newsletter, I wrote:

Dear Friends

This time last year we were rejoicing in David's successful kidney transplant. We looked forward to the freeing of time spent dialysing each day, and greater strength and vigour. I had booked a holiday in Austria, camping with Euro Camp – we love camping and walking, as you know. Also, the challenging task of refurbishing the church had been completed, and we were ready to move towards Alpha courses and the like.

But all this was not to be. David had first a kidney infection then a respiratory infection which developed into pneumonia from which he died in February. This was quite unexpected and, with so many people praying for him, seems impossible to understand. Kidney transplant patients do sometimes lose their new kidney, but this usually means going back onto dialysis.

May I thank you for your prayers, cards and support received. There were so many cards and letters that my daughter Ann, my son Graham and I divided them up each morning and opened them together, reading them out to one another, marvelling at the number of lives David had touched, and crying together. One card said, 'Those who die in grace go no further from us than God, and God is very near.'

The thanksgiving/funeral service was extraordinary. David had a gift with special services, making them relevant, joyful occasions. We prayed that this service would be one of faith and joy, knowing that David was released from pain, had accomplished his work and was with the Lord. The church was full, with standing room only, and the atmosphere of faith, hope and thanksgiving was wonderful, many of you having travelled a long way to be with us. Thank you for coming.

David's unexpected death brought shock. As time went on, I became more fully aware of all I had lost. Above all, there was the loss of my husband after twenty-nine years of very happy marriage. But there were other losses too. Loss of job – for I had worked alongside David in the church. Loss of identity – since I was no longer the vicar's wife. Loss of home – because the vicarage had to be vacated for the next incumbent. And, last but not least, loss of my vicar – since David had been that to me as well.

I think back to that strange moment when hope went and death arrived. Graham, Ann and I went to see David in the intensive care room, after all the pipes had been removed and all the equipment taken away. On opening the door, I involuntarily exclaimed, 'Oh, it's like a morgue!' The change from life to death is so stark. Looking at David we saw a gentle, peaceful expression and a half-smile on his face. We were glad that his suffering was over; glad in the knowledge that he had faithfully served God, us and the church. But desolate in the knowledge that we had lost a loving friend as well as husband and father.

In planning the funeral service, which we called a thanksgiving service, Graham, his fiancée Kate, and Ann and I looked at favourite hymns and Bible passages. We also had to make decisions about the music and about who would take the service, lead the prayers and preach. I typed out the hymns and programme, Kate copied a lovely line-drawing illustrating our chosen psalm, a friend transferred it all to the desk-top publishing option, and we all went to another vicarage to photocopy and staple the result. Having so many tasks to complete in the first week helped us to share with each other and with friends and other relatives memories of many happy occasions, as well as our trust in God and our confidence that David was enjoying eternal life with Jesus and his saints.

After the funeral director called, the bishop came to see me. We talked of David, the family, my plans. Amazing as it may seem, we even laughed together. I spoke of a funny incident which the bishop capped with a story which was even funnier. What my mother thought about this hilarity, I don't know!

As I look back at the sequence of events leading up to David's death, many mysteries remain. David had been longing for a transplant in the hope that it would greatly improve his quality of life. I had been more nervous about the possibility – it would involve pain and the chance of rejection, which in turn would mean the use of very strong drugs, with side-effects and more suffering. David had been passing blood for ten days, and was in bed with severe kidney pain when the call from the hospital came. It was then the afternoon of 5th November 1994. Gaining strength from the adrenalin released by the hope of a transplant, he managed to get up and I took him to the hospital.

The waiting room seemed to be charged with a sense of the momentous. I waited for David to be examined. Another family group visiting a relative broke off their conversation to ask whether David was the Reverend Bottley, who had been very kind to them in the past. Finding out that he was, they wished us well.

I rang people at church to pray for the right decisions to be made. As it was bonfire night, relays of people left the fire and went into the church hall to pray. They were all aware of David's desire to have a transplant and of some of the potential problems. The worst that anyone could envisage were the trauma and pain of kidney rejection if that were to occur.

Normally a transplant would not even be considered for a patient with any sort of infection, so I could not understand the delay in decision making. David kept hoping that the operation would take place and I believed that if it were to go ahead, it would be because God was answering the prayers of so many of us.

As we waited for the outcome, David and I talked, held hands, ignored the television in the corner, tried to read magazines, sighed at regular intervals, got up and walked around. How long can an evening last!

Finally a doctor came in. Yes, he would do the transplant, he said. He would also remove the right kidney which was causing so much pain. As I understand it, kidneys are not easy to take out, since they are tucked behind the ribs to give them some protection from damage. Transplanted kidneys, however, are placed more accessibly in the groin.

Waving goodbye to David as he was whisked away on the trolley was one of the hardest things I have ever had to do. I wept my way to the car. But there was soon some good news – the new kidney worked immediately, which is not often the case. The old kidney had been huge, as big as a rugby ball, and was definitely better out than in.

In ten days David was home. The antibiotic was changed

from intravenous to tablet form. A new regime began for me at home. Temperature, pulse and blood pressure had to be taken twice a day, recorded and telephoned in. The very next day, David was ill and had to return to hospital with a severe kidney infection perhaps from the original kidney. I spent all the following afternoons and evenings with David. These were very happy and contented times of being together. We had always enjoyed each other's company, and through working together we had had a lot of it. But this was a sharing of a different kind. There was one mealtime which I particularly remember when the quality of our fellowship was even more special. It was as if God had anointed it, and we both felt the presence of Jesus there with us. 'To be in your presence, not rushing away; to cherish each moment, here I would stay.' The words of that song captured something of what we experienced together, which was, I believe, a foretaste of our fellowship with Jesus in heaven. Sometimes now I find it hard to sing those particular words in worship.

After ten days, David was home again, with the kidney working well and everyone predicting an increase in strength and a return to work in February. Subsequent regular visits to the hospital revealed perfect kidney function, but I was worried about David and kept asking when he would actually seem better. Although the staff had also expected him to be stronger by then, they still seemed to be focusing all their attention on his kidney.

On one visit I remember asking, 'Where is all his energy going?' adding, 'He is eating more than I've ever known him to but he's still losing weight. There must be an infection somewhere.' He was also, I noticed, getting more breathless. The doctors didn't want to give David antibiotics. They said that they needed to identify the virus in order to target it accurately, and that in any case antibiotics wouldn't have much effect because of the anti-rejection drugs he was on.

The week before David had to return to hospital again was 'hunt the virus' time. He attended the kidney unit for tests three times. Nothing could be identified, they said, adding, 'But his kidney is working well.' By this time we were not very interested in the kidney: David had done better on dialysis.

One night, David could hardly breathe. Half-blinded by my tears, I dragged a mattress and bed down and set it up in the dining room. I was scared and bewildered. Where was this all going to lead? Why was David so ill? He had been home over Christmas, but it had been obvious to everyone then that all was not well.

That night David's kidney stopped working. I drove him back to hospital where he was seen by two consultants. They diagnosed pneumonia. I was assured that people rarely die of pneumonia nowadays, and that they might be able to save the kidney.

My children, Graham, Ann and Stephen, as well as Ann's husband and my mother and sister, were all able to stay with me at home and at the hospital for various lengths of time. During David's last four days in intensive care, we were given a room in which Ann and I slept and showered and received day visitors who wanted to spend time with us. Friends in the parish brought casseroles, puddings, fruit. Various clergy found their way there, and an assurance of people's prayers from all over the country made this time even more intensive and extraordinary.

Just how much can a day hold? Here's how I spent the second Sunday after David's funeral.

8.00 am   Showered, washed hair, had breakfast. Made Mum comfortable in front room with food, tablets, duvet and magazines. She wanted to hear the funeral service while I was out at church. She liked it and said it was a good recording, much to my relief as I had not managed to listen to the tapes I'd copied.

10.30 am	Church – Brownie Parade. Saw Carolyn's new baby, just six weeks old. Jim and Dorothy are very proud grandparents. Baby fast asleep – looked as peaceful as David did when he was sedated. These unexpected happenings really ruin any self-control.
1.30 pm	Cottage pie and sprouts – very nice. Hazel rang: Would I like to go out for a walk? We went to Stannington and walked over an area known as Twenty Fields. Nearly finished the walk when I cried again – first time I had been walking without David. Funny how one minute I can be talking and laughing and the next crying deep, heartfelt tears.
4.30 pm	Called in at the Hopkins to return dish. Had coffee and some gorgeous fruit cake. Picked up Bryan, saw hall decorations and returned to vicarage. Made omelettes. Hazel supplied and prepared salad. We enjoyed Pat's chocolate cake. My sister Hazel rang from her hotel room in Austria, enquiring after Mum and me. Mum had a better night but is still in a lot of pain.
6.30 pm	Communion – enjoyable till the administration. Suddenly aware that David should be doing it. Had to hand everything to Jesus at the rail, accept his will for my life and ask his blessing and peace.
7.45 pm	Hazel took me home, threading through the fair and all the Supertram works. Stephen rang – had a good talk. Rang Ruth about thank-you cards. Read her the wording and she said she would send me samples and then run off about 200 initially. Hope that is more than enough!

After David's death, there were many practical matters to discuss. Where was I to live? Should I move to be near relatives? But they were scattered around the country and my children might well move at some time in the future from where they were. Should I stay in the parish and go to the same church? I had been there for twenty years and our children had grown up there alongside the families of our friends. Together, we had become like an extended family. How could I leave? But, equally, how could I bear to stay and see another family in the vicarage and another vicar leading the church?

Two days after the funeral, Mum, Ann, Graham and I visited friends, who put forward the idea that we should go and take a look at their old house which was available for rent. The suggestion took me by surprise. It seemed too soon to be having to look at property. But my friends knew that I would soon be on my own in the vicarage, and wondered whether I might then find it hard to motivate myself to go house-hunting. So we looked at the house, then bought a local property guide and ordered brochures. The search for my new home was on.

It seemed sensible to remain in Sheffield where my friends were, and even to remain in the same church, provided that the next vicar and wife were happy about it. Our family was praying for guidance and many others were holding us in their prayers at this time.

I moved into my new home five months after David's death. One of my regrets about this is that David has not seen it and never will. The Lord wonderfully provided it for me and I would love David to know of this and of the other evidences of his love and care. And what about my new ministry – does David know about that? I believe that he does.

How did my new work and role come about? Through attending as usual the annual Good News Trust convention. For nine years I had been co-ordinator of the Sheffield Good News van – a mobile Christian library service, taking books, tapes and videos for borrowing to homes where friends and neighbours have gathered at the invitation of their owners. This is a wonderful, non-threatening form of evangelism as well as a resource for Christians. There are thirty-four vans scattered throughout the British Isles and Eire.

I knew the convention would prove to be an emotional time for me. Many of the teams had been praying for David for years, and would be very sympathetic. However, it was good to be among friends and share in the usual seminars and worship times. At one point, the chairman of the trustees explained all the different responsibilities involved in the working of the trust, and also informed us of various vacancies. I did not pay a great deal of attention for most of what was being said was for the benefit of people new to the trust. But what concerned everyone was that we were still praying for a person to replace our director, who was retiring the following year.

To my astonishment, three people approached me about the position. I quickly informed them that I appear to be more intelligent and capable than I actually am and could not possibly take on such a task, although I was honoured that they should have considered me. My words fell on deaf ears and, as one of three was the current director and founder of the trust, I felt I had to agree at least to pray about the matter and discuss it with those who knew me well.

I knew that doing this work would involve a steep learning curve for me, both spiritually and in terms of having to learn or develop new skills. Producing a monthly news and prayer letter, organising a national convention, moving the office to Sheffield, caring for and visiting all the teams annually and promoting the trust – all this would pose an enormous challenge. How much easier it would have been to settle in my new home, go to church, lead ongoing Alpha groups and continue my work with the bookstall and local Good News van. Surely that would have been quite enough for me to manage, especially while going through a bereavement.

But, as I was to prove, God is in the business of growth and development. After much prayer and consultation, I accepted the appointment, and on the following day, I 'saw' a huge head and shoulders of David, filling two thirds of the sky. He had a big grin on his face and was holding one hand aloft as he said, 'Hallelujah, praise the Lord! That's my girl, and you're gorgeous.' 'That's my girl,' was a phrase I can't remember David using much but the other phrases he certainly said often. Before then other people had 'seen' David – in church or in a dream. But I never had. His going had seemed so total and final. But then I had this vision, which, as far as I was concerned, set a seal of approval on my new life.

Having ascertained God's will, accepted it and started on my responsibilities, I am discovering a new identity of my own. Also I have found that the Lord has given me ideas during my quiet times and sent me people with skills at just the right times. And it has been a great joy for me to travel round the country meeting lovely Christian people involved in reaching out to and serving others via the Good News vans.

Sometimes I get very tired: in fact, I have never known such depths of tiredness as those I experienced during the first year of my bereavement. I still have a lot to organise in order to make my task easier, as well as presentations to prepare to enable me to publicise the trust more effectively. Even so, at the moment, I am feeling a little more relaxed in my new role.

For the most part, life is made up of little things. One of those for me was having to deal with the answer-phone which had David's voice on it. It would be less distressing to have a different voice delivering the message. I could not bear the idea of recording over David's voice. In fact, in my shock, I couldn't even conjure up the sound of his voice in my mind. Anyway, we bought another tape. Also, I began to hunt for tape recordings of our church services. These were lent to the house-bound then returned for reuse. I got hold of a few of these, but they were only labelled with the date of the recording, so I didn't know just by looking at them whether David's voice would be on them or not.

It was a long time before I plucked up courage to listen to a tape, not knowing how it would affect me if I were to hear David's voice. In fact, I loved it. I have always enjoyed David's preaching and it was so comforting to hear it again. I especially like him leading the congregation in the creed: he so obviously believed in what he was saying. Nowadays, I very rarely listen to a tape, but simply knowing that I can remind myself of the sound of David's voice imparting his faith is a treasure.

Everything seems more intense since David died. Somehow the deep pain and anguish is matched with an equally deep enjoyment. The beauty of the countryside near my home; flowers and shrubs; sunsets and night skies; the seaside and friendships; reading the Bible and experiencing God's presence: everything appears more vital and alive. I don't understand why this should be, but I heard the same point made by English people living in Columbia when they were interviewed by the BBC. They said that the danger involved in living where they do causes them to relish and embrace life all the more fully. Perhaps our senses are dulled when life is easy or, at least, less challenging.

I have a much lower than normal concentration level for thinking, doing, listening, talking, and my energy – emotional and physical – is low. My feelings are difficult to assess. They seem normal most of the time. But then emotions can build up and erupt like steam from a pressure-cooker. During a service shortly after the funeral, I began to feel panic and needed help to get outside into the fresh air. There in the garden I began to scream and scream and stamp my feet. I had never done this before. Fortunately I remembered seeing people undergoing similar experiences at a John Wimber conference or some other gathering. This reassured me that I was not going mad: merely releasing the tension, anger, and frustration that had been building up inside over the past few months. My friends were not phased by my behaviour. They provided a chair, said kind things and brought tea when I had calmed down. Soon I rejoined the service, and was able to drive home afterwards. I felt emotionally tired but believed that anger and frustration buried in my subconscious had been released. Later I was able to examine this experience and pray about it with our new vicar and a friend, and this brought me further healing and peace.

I believe worship is part of the Lord's provision for us. We are more vulnerable and open then, so that our emotional needs, or our need for confession, forgiveness, cleansing and so on, are more able to rise to the surface. In more and more churches nowadays, people are available to minister God's love and grace, forgiveness and healing.

It surprises me that life still goes on and one can laugh and joke. Then comes the sudden awareness of loss, evoked by a hug, a walk, a service such as communion, the sight of couples, peaceful babies or grandads enjoying grandchildren.

As far as the Bible is concerned, I have always enjoyed reading the book of Isaiah – the good bits anyway – but now I am really begining to like and appreciate Isaiah himself: the courage and the poetry in the man. When reading the writings of Paul or Peter, I find myself saying, 'Good for you, Paul!' or, 'Go for it, Peter!' Strangely enough, I find it harder to read Christ's words in the Gospels. They take such a lot of meditation and working out.

Sometimes, after having a great time with my Bible reading, guitar playing and singing, I drive off to church expecting a wonderful time of worship there. But one word of a chorus is all it takes to turn joy to grief. At other times, I skimp on my quiet time, or find it hard and unproductive, or just feel really miserable. Not wanting to make other people feel miserable or sorry for me, I start wondering whether I should stay at home rather than go to church. But in the end I go, and what happens? The Lord draws near and restores my soul.

'All things work together for good' (Romans 8:28). Graham rang shocked and angry: he had been made redundant. It was unexpected, and to his mind, unnecessary. But on reflection, this only brought forward by a year his own career plan. He wanted to get a PGCE for teaching music and to attend Bretton Hall College near Barnsley which had an excellent reputation for music and the arts. His redundancy occurred in July, a week before I moved. My new house is a mere nineteen miles from the college. Graham helped me move, brought his own furniture over from Leighton Buzzard, gained an interview at the college and began his course in the September.

It has been so lovely for me to have him here for a year. He is so much like his father in looks and in his sense of humour. He misses his dad, and it has been good to be able to talk about him and the things we did together. His fiancée Kate is studying at Leeds University, so it is much more convenient for him to be in Sheffield. He would have had to spend much time and money in travelling had he stayed in Leighton Buzzard.

Since David died, I have adopted the policy of accepting invitations and going out to things, without worrying too much about my unpredictable reactions. Whether it's to a church service, a bishop's garden party, a prayer meeting, ten-pin bowling or walking – I go to it. I make the decision at home and leave the consequences in God's hands.

One day, I was invited to attend a strawberry soirée – whatever that meant! In fact, it was a garden party for clergy, wives, husbands and people like me – I still recoil at being designated a widow. We were to bring a sweet or drink with strawberry ingredients. There was to be croquet on one lawn and racquets for other games would be placed in other locations. A music quartet was to entertain us. It all sounded very civilised. I wanted to go, and knew that

David would have loved it. In fact, I want to go to lots of things because they have been my way of life: not just garden parties, of course, but events in which I can share with others the joys and challenges of the type of work we do. But the questions which arise when I receive such invitations are: Will I be upset by seeing people mainly in couples and by receiving condolences? Will I be an embarrassment if I should cry? Have I the right to go to these events now or am I out of place – trying to hang on when I should be letting go? Will people be thinking, 'Whatever is she doing here?'

Despite such questions and in keeping with my new philosophy, I went to the soirée – and enjoyed it. Surprisingly perhaps, I spent a good proportion of the time sharing how God had provided me first with a home and then with a ministry; and how he had also arranged things so that my eldest son would be able to live with me for a year. The person to whom I was speaking for much of the time was a clergy wife who was obviously worried about what would happen to her if her husband should die. So it was good to be so positive about the Lord's care, as well as about what is offered by the church commissioners and pension board. The church authorities, it seems to me, have taken seriously the requirement to care for widows and orphans, and nowadays there is financial help and advice readily available and kindly offered to us.

Of course, deciding what to do when anniversaries come around is much harder. Then I may take myself off to bed, which, for me, is a comfort and escape. Or I may arrange an alternative activity. On bonfire night, for example, I had a few people around for a meal, and the occasion was a success, even though I had got out of the habit of cooking and a few unimportant mishaps occurred!

For some time I had been aware of the fact that I had some unfinished business to attend to. David had died in February. He had often said to me that when he died he wanted his ashes scattered on the top of Winn Hill. This would involve a long, steep climb up from Yorkshire Bridge, and my response had always been that I hoped that I would be too old and decrepit to be able to do that. But after David had died, I mentioned the matter one day to Graham and he said that his father had said the same thing to him. So we agreed that the task had to be done and Graham volunteered to accompany me. We told Ann and Stephen about the plan, and they were happy to let us do as David had wished. Time went by until our wedding anniversary came up one Sunday in August. Graham was with me, and as I didn't feel I could face going to church that day, we decided to climb the hill.

I wanted to carry the ashes as my last physical service to David. But they proved to be very heavy, and feeling tired and having to climb in very windy, wet weather made matters worse. So we shared in the task. At the top, we tried to find shelter behind some rocks, away from nosy sheep. There we read some appropriate paragraphs and psalms from the Prayer Book and gave thanks for David's life. Then we scattered his ashes. I expected them to fly away, borne on the wind. But they proved to be hard white chippings which fell to the ground. After my initial surprise, I felt happy about that. It seemed even more satisfactory to me that they should remain on the ground along part of one of our favourite walking routes. It was good too that I was with Graham who had occasionally joined us on our walks when he'd been on holiday from university or work. Grief is experienced by all the family, and what Graham really misses are discussing issues and sharing friendship with his father.

Because of my belief in the power of prayer and in spiritual healing, the way David died raised some heartsearing questions for me. If it had been David's time to be with the Lord, why the transplant, especially at a time when he had been so ill? Had that been an example of human error? Yet our church had specifically prayed on bonfire night that the decision and all the circumstances would be right. But I was able to draw strength from my years of knowing God and his faithfulness towards us. And I knew that what had happened had not been brought about by any lack of faith or of prayer on our part. The presence of God remained very real throughout.

I believe too that it's not so much what happens to us in life that is important, but how we respond to it. In this connection I found something Eddie Askew wrote very helpful. In describing how Canada geese behaved when 'their environment had suddenly become hostile, threatening', he says, 'They didn't protest or run for cover. They didn't use up precious energy flying into it, or fighting it. They faced into the wind, paddling quietly. They didn't try to make headway, but paddled just enough to keep their direction and position in the water.'

Over and above all this was the deep conviction that God is all powerful; that nothing can happen without his permission. I did not like what was happening one bit but it is at such times that faith is tested. What was tested for me was not so much my faith in God himself but in his ability to comfort and sustain me; faith not just as a system of belief to get us through life, but the knowledge and assurance that when the chips are down, God is there with us as a reality. His answer to our prayers was not what we wanted or hoped for, which would have given rise to unmitigated joy and praise. True, in David's death we have the joy of knowing that his pain is over, that he has run a good race, and is in heaven with all the company of believers. But of course we have also grief and pain – and questions.

Some questions I refuse to torment myself with: those relating to the wisdom and timing of the transplant and the possibility of human error there or in the after-care David was given. Nothing can bring David back. The kidney unit will have learnt hard lessons from what happened; after all, the last thing they would have wanted was their patient's death. Besides, I believe that God is all powerful and ultimately in control and so, bearing in mind too that many people were praying for us, the outcome must have been, in some mysterious way, within his will. Accepting this, I believe, will be the quickest way to my healing. I know that I will have to make continual acts of acceptance before I experience healing and wholeness as a continuous reality in my life. I hold on to God's promise in Jeremiah 29:11 – '"For I know the plans I have for you," declares the Lord, "plans to prosper you and not to harm you, plans to give you hope and a future."'

Other questions in my mind are about what our relationships will be like in heaven. I have become an avid reader of books on death and bereavement mainly because of wanting answers to such questions. In the Bible, the story of Jesus' transfiguration indicates that Moses and Elijah, though separated by centuries when they lived on earth, know and are able to communicate with each other in heaven. I find that encouraging. But what am I to make of Jesus' teaching that there will be no marriage in heaven? Will David and I still be special to each other when we meet there? If so, in what way? I don't know the answers to those and other questions. But I do know that, in the present, I really miss the mutual belonging and utter acceptance David and I experienced in our marriage; and I am learning to wait on the Lord to bring me to a position of being complete in and fully satisfied by him.

Trevor's Story

Trevor Jones lives in Sevenoaks, Kent, and works for BT. He has a daughter, Charlotte, aged nineteen, and a son, Nicholas, aged seventeen.

Trevor's story was written two years and four months after the death of his wife Diana.

I have never found it easy to cry and could probably recount every time in the last thirty years when I have actually wept, my more usual reaction being a very painful lump in the throat until the unwelcome feeling goes away. 'Typical man!' I can almost hear you saying but, believe me, it would have been a lot more comforting and releasing at times if my tears could have flowed more readily.

Trevor's Story

Diana and I moved to Sevenoaks in 1981 and became Christians some time in 1983. We had both been church-goers until our teens but had then drifted away; although we had both been confirmed in the Church of England, we did not have a strong faith. We started going to church again when we wanted the children to go to Sunday school, Diana having encountered some very helpful people at the church school. She and I had met in January 1970 and married in 1972, Charlotte arriving after quite a struggle in 1977, Nick making his presence known after even more of a fight two years later.

It was in January 1989 that our doctor made an urgent appointment for a mammogram for Diana. This was to be the first of many shocks, challenges and surprises that we were to face in the next five years. The trouble started when Diana found what felt like the tip of a point in her left breast. How we had managed to miss it earlier was unbelievable, given the extent of the tumour soon found by the surgeon, and given also Diana's very slim figure. The mammogram, which took place three days after seeing the GP, revealed a multi-faceted tumour and within a week Diana was undergoing a lumpectomy. The biopsy which followed showed that the tumour was malignant and aggressive, so our surgeon recommended a complete mastectomy. This was something we agreed to go ahead with, after praying with the surgeon. No, we weren't that bold as Christians; it just happened that the surgeon to whom we were referred is a Christian and a member of our church! There is a lot of debate about the treatment of breast cancer and I have neither the knowledge nor desire to enter that discussion. Suffice it to say that we had every confidence in the person advising us and, after prayer, accepted his advice.

A week later Diana was back in hospital having a radical mastectomy. The weeks that followed were difficult, as she went through a kind of mourning for the loss of her breast, as well as suffering from the after-effects of major surgery. More bad news was given to us a couple of weeks after the operation: the cancer had spread to the lymph nodes under the left arm and as many as possible had been removed during the operation. The surgeon was very honest in assessing the likelihood of more nodes being affected and we certainly felt that the operation had been just in time. While Diana was still in hospital for the second time, my optimism about the future took a severe denting as all we seemed to be hearing was negative and worrying. I remember coming away from the hospital with the children, Charlotte and Nick, aged eleven and nine respectively at the time, and being very open in telling them that their mummy might not live very long. It was one of those things which I regretted as soon as it was said but the children took it very well and it might have helped in the years which followed.

Although Diana and I had been Christians since 1982, we had not learned to pray together very easily and our belief in God's healing power was very much in relation to the past rather than as something which could be experienced in the present. However, we did pray for peace and Diana certainly wanted to live. Like many women, she was courageous, someone who never gave up but rather kept going in all circumstances. This attitude had sometimes been a challenge to me, especially when she would soldier on through flu, bronchitis and other ailments, refusing to see a doctor or have treatment until she really could not cope. Perhaps she was a bit 'head in the sand' about her own illnesses at times. Did she initially ignore any little signs of a lump in her breast? I don't know but I hope I shall find that out when we meet again!

Diana was determined to live, as she wanted to be sure the children were brought up properly and to see them through their education. Determination and a growing dependence on God and his promises were features of the rest of 1989 as she underwent radiotherapy, bone scans and the effects of burns from the treatment. Our house at times contained more plants and flowers than some of the local garden centres and the walls of the hall were covered with get-well cards of every shape and size. The love and concern of our friends was overwhelming and there was never a shortage of volunteers to take Diana on the twenty-minute journey to the hospital for radiotherapy. Whenever she was too tired to cook, there was always a meal for us organised by one of the support groups from the church.

As the burns began to heal and Diana's strength returned, we had another decision to make – one which has given me anxiety at times ever since. It was usual to undergo a course of chemotherapy following breast cancer even if radiotherapy was prescribed. However, we had heard so many terrible stories about 'chemo' that Diana was very reluctant to go through the further suffering which would probably result. Our GP advised that chemotherapy would probably only increase by ten per cent Diana's survival chances. We talked, prayed and even argued a bit, but the final decision, which had to be Diana's, was to go without the treatment.

We had been told that if a breast cancer patient survives for four years after the initial treatment, he or she has as much chance as anyone else of reaching old age. This hope kept us going for the next few years although the thought that Diana might be on borrowed time did occasionally cross our minds. However, we had a pretty normal life and Diana was in full swing working at a local coffee shop run by Christians, playing badminton and running the crèche at our church on Sunday mornings. My parent's golden wedding in 1993 was a happy occasion and one of the best photographs of Diana and me was taken at the time.

During 1993 Diana had been having frequent sore throats and generally not feeling too good at times, but we did not associate it with anything serious as she had always been susceptible to such infections. However, just before Christmas she began to feel little lumps in her neck and across her shoulders. After a mix-up over her test results, which worried Diana a great deal, we asked to be referred to Guy's Hospital and soon knew that the lumps were secondary cancer.

Then started a series of lows and highs. Initial tests showed that the cancer did not appear to be anywhere else, so the new regime of treatment involved radiotherapy to the affected areas. Then further scans indicated that there was more cancer in the chest area. But worse was to follow. During one of the scans of the chest, the radiographer thought he saw some disease in the top of the liver which was just visible. So back Diana went for a full liver scan. This confirmed that there were three or four areas of disease. It sounded like a death sentence and was probably the biggest challenge to our faith that we had encountered.

Why would God allow Diana to go through all that and still let her face more suffering? Surely he wouldn't let such a lovely person and strong Christian endure so much and then die? What purpose would that serve? All these questions and more were spinning round our thoughts and prayers most of the time. I still do not have an answer to them. Indeed, I have felt very angry at times; angry with God for letting it all happen; angry with myself for not insisting on chemotherapy at the beginning; angry with Diana for not wanting treatment and yet wanting to be healed.

The anger and frustration in both of us blew up one lovely morning in the summer. I was hanging out the washing at the time and had decided to hang a pair of jeans from the waist instead of upside down from the legs which was what Diana always did. Seeing what I was doing, she said the job should be done her way. You will have to imagine the kind of tension there can be in such situations, if you have not experienced it. 'Perfect' human beings no doubt would have reacted differently! Not being perfect myself, I was decidedly put out, and Diana and I exchanged a few hasty words which resulted in her being in tears and me feeling as though I were contributing directly to the spread of her cancer. After an appropriate stand-off, we both managed to apologise, and things got back to 'normal'. Thankfully, Diana had a lot of support from her Christian friends who would come to pray with her at a moment's notice. This helped us both as she had an escape route whenever we were unable to help each other out of difficult times.

Prayer groups and prayer chains played an increasing part in Diana's life and she became more aware of the possibility of healing by God. From the time of the diagnosis of secondary cancer, she had been trying to find out more about healing and had read several books containing impressive anecdotal evidence. We also heard of instances reported by Christian friends and acquaintances and so we began to pray a great deal with friends and also to visit churches and Christian healing centres where healing had been experienced. Now, as I read through Diana's diary and notes – something she said I could do – I am reminded of how convinced she was that God would heal her. Those who prayed with her also were sure she would live. Much of the time I too believed she could be healed and we often prayed together for her healing. In fact, when the children or I prayed and laid hands on Diana, her pain would often be relieved, which we found very encouraging. But sadly the effects didn't go beyond short-term pain relief. However, Diana still firmly believed that she was going to get better and go on living.

Chemotherapy started in June 1994 and the effects were as bad as feared. The strongest possible drugs were being given, in an effort to destroy the cancer in the liver. After about four sessions of chemotherapy, things did not seem to be getting any better, so in August we saw the consultant and he agreed that further treatment was unlikely to be effective. We decided to commit the whole thing to God and to trust him. This was a great step of faith and it was also a relief for Diana to be free of worry about the awful side-effects of the chemotherapy.

In July we joined a group of friends from our church who were going on a houseparty to the Isle of Wight. Diana was desperate to go but I went reluctantly. She felt that she had to be prepared to go anywhere in order to receive healing; I, on the other hand, didn't think that a week in typical boarding school accommodation would do anything for her comfort. Also I felt sure that I would not enjoy a week of 'happy clappy' services! On the way down to Portsmouth on the hottest day we had experienced so far that year, we had reason to thank God for the car air-conditioning which every other member of the family had mocked as being yuppie or soft. It was to prove a blessing on many other occasions too. As Diana's disease progressed, sometimes the air-conditioned car was the only place where she could feel comfortable and breathe with some degree of ease. The holiday, too, proved to be good and we met some lovely people who were a great support during the week and also afterwards through letters and prayer.

At a healing service just prior to the holiday, it had been

suggested by someone that I should give Diana into Jesus' care and I think doing this, and accepting my anxiety that she might not be healed, enabled me to begin to grieve. It was also a kind of healing experience for me, in that it freed me to concentrate on caring for Diana rather than striving for her healing. During the subsequent houseparty I felt able to receive support from others and experienced a sense of peace and strength from their prayers. This holiday was also my first exposure to some of the 'charismatic things' about which I had previously felt uncomfortable. During one of the group discussions we were asked to pray for each other and ask for healing. In this session the group felt very strongly that I needed prayer. 'Oh no!' was my instinctive thought. But some people proceeded to pray and lay hands on me, and I had a very strong sense of peace and release and found myself laughing gently for several minutes. I found the experience very helpful. For the rest of the holiday we received wonderful teaching and ministry. The downside was that Diana felt very poorly and spent a lot of time in bed.

Then, on the ferry returning to Portsmouth, Diana's hair started to fall out. This is a common side-effect of chemotherapy but it still came as a bit of a shock, for Diana had already had her last treatment. The free wig, which we already had, was brought into action as more of Diana's hair came out with each brushing. I came home from work one day and found Diana sitting in her usual place.

'I've got something to show you,' she said and whisked off her wig to reveal a totally hairless head. I was taken aback for a few moments but she and Nick thought it was a good joke so we all had a laugh! Diana explained that she'd got bored with her hair falling out gradually, and so she and Nick had speeded the process by removing it forcibly. This brought a new element into my grieving: Diana's hair had always been attractive and it seemed as if a bit of her had already gone for ever. I couldn't help wishing she hadn't hastened the loss of this aspect of herself. She kept the remains of her hair in a supermarket carrier bag, but this didn't really soften the sense of finality for me.

Soon after this we had one of our last consultations at Guy's Hospital, but we continued to go there in connection with problems associated with the spread of the cancer. The unpleasantness of that last consultation caused anger, grief and to some extent a strain on the relationship between Diana and myself, which had been very good – give or take the fact that neither of us was perfect!

The consultant we saw on that occasion was someone we had not previously seen. He noticed that Diana was carrying a book on Christian healing and proceeded to set about deriding any belief in healing. He also told us that he would not have allowed us to stop treatment if we had been seen by his 'firm'. He was extremely blunt and said that Diana would only have a few months to live. We left the hospital in a state of terrible turmoil. I felt that this really was the end and I also wished I had punched the consultant on the nose or done something a lot worse. At this stage Diana was having to get about in a wheelchair most of the time and I remember pushing her along the river bank towards Tower Bridge and feeling utterly miserable. Diana felt the same but her emotions boiled over in a tirade against the designer of the river wall for making it so high that someone in a wheelchair couldn't see over it. I don't know whether her resolve to be healed was strengthened or damaged by the consultant's unfeeling words but she continued to look for a miracle. By contrast, I believed increasingly that Diana was not going to receive what she desperately wanted.

As a result, I began to feel a mixture of anger and despair along with deep love and sadness. I wanted to talk about the future but felt unable to do so much of the time; and I would have loved to have done things which we had always talked about doing before Diana became too weak, but I couldn't do so as long as she was absorbed with her healing and its aftermath. Instead I began to try to face up to what life would be like without Diana. Although this was painful, I think it may have helped in my overall grieving.

At about this time, I began to experience feelings of pointlessness. Knowing, as I felt I did, that Diana would die soon, seemed to make everything we tried to do futile. Diana's diaries and notes, on the other hand, reveal in the main that she was still very positive and expectant – an indication, perhaps, that I managed to hide my feelings from her in this respect at least.

During October one of the best events to date happened, giving us both a lift. A group of friends had already been holding prayer vigils round the clock for us during particularly difficult times and they now organised a worship and prayer service which included about sixty people from five local churches and a range of differing denominations. At one point in the service, Diana was totally surrounded by people praying over her and laying their hands on her. She experienced incredibly deep peace, but still no sign of healing. However, other good things happened. A number of people with strained or broken relationships were reconciled to one another and, as I understand it, have remained friends ever since. I have often wondered whether it was God's will that Diana's life and situation should do good in such ways.

By the end of October, Diana was having difficulty with most activities and had to be carried up and down the stairs. I was given indefinite compassionate leave, since looking after Diana had become a full-time job even with the constant provision of cooked evening meals from our friends. Once again the house had become a horticultural centre and the walls could hardly be seen for the cards from friends and acquaintances. I think that the level of support we received was a major contributory factor in keeping me going. To know that practical and prayer help was only a phone call away at any time was the back-up I couldn't have done without.

My grieving started in earnest about two weeks before Diana died, when I found that I could hardly look at her without feelings of sadness, regret, pity and loss. By this time I had given up all hope of healing. I have never found it easy to cry and could probably recount every time in the last thirty years when I have actually wept, my more usual reaction being a very painful lump in the throat until the unwelcome feeling goes away. 'Typical man!' I can almost hear you saying but, believe me, it would have been a lot more comforting and releasing at times if my tears could have flowed more readily. But it's not something you can force. However, I remember one evening when I was sitting by the bed and feeling so low that I put my arms round Diana and cried on her shoulder for several minutes. She was too weak to talk much but she held me as tightly as she could and I knew that this would probably be our last time of sharing intimacy and affection. I felt as though I were having to say goodbye to all the love and tenderness we had enjoyed over twenty-two years of marriage. It was a terrible experience. It occurred to me later that losing a loved one after an illness at least makes for a more gradual separation. I can't imagine how it must be to cope with the sudden death of someone very close.

The house was seldom without a visitor coming with food, flowers and good wishes or to pray with Diana. Sometimes I felt a little hurt that very few people appeared to have concern for how I was managing, as I rushed around doing the chores. The feeling was intensified a few weeks after Diana's death when I was sure the phone had been disconnected and the postman kidnapped. It was as if a tap had been turned off and I felt very lonely and upset. I know people were wanting to respect my privacy but it felt as if I had been abandoned now that Diana had gone. This was no doubt irrational – for meals continued to arrive every evening, until I decided that I had to do the dinner myself – but a genuine feeling I had at that time nonetheless.

Diana died on 20th November 1994 at the age of forty-seven. From then until the middle of January was a period of numbness marked by a great deal of activity, for tasks needing to be done were very numerous.

The biggest event was, of course, the service. We had a small family service at the crematorium in the morning followed by a memorial and thanksgiving service at a 'borrowed' church in the afternoon: our own church building was closed for major works and had a large hole where its floor had once been.

Planning the service was both a joy and a nightmare. A joy because of all the people who were willing to help. It was easy to arrange for people to do the readings and prayers. We wanted to make the service fresh and joyful without causing offence to anyone who might feel that such occasions should be sombre and funereal. Diana had said she wanted people to rejoice that she was with God. But trying to make her wishes a reality led to emotional exchanges between the three of us. Nick wanted to include many of the songs and choruses we had learned on the houseparty and did not want any traditional hymns. Charlotte did not want anything new, as she had not been on the houseparty and was more conservative. I was trying to steer a course down the middle for the sake of peace and out of consideration for any who might feel uncomfortable about having to try and sing unfamiliar songs.

We had several discussions which became more and more agitated as the deadline for arrangements drew near. The worst behaviour was displayed by myself one evening when I became so angry that I threw my copy of the church song book across the lounge. It hit the French window frame and burst in a flurry of pages around the room. Yes, I was sorry and no, I couldn't admit it at once. However, we all calmed down a bit after that, apologies were offered and we soon had the book back together and the final decisions made.

The memorial service did all come together and was a lovely tribute to Diana's faith, love and care. There must have been more than 400 people present, many of whom had no faith and only associated church with old-fashioned words and strange rituals. One tough business man said he would not have believed that there could be such a sense of happiness at a funeral. Had the service been one of thanksgiving for Diana's healing, it might have been attended only by Christians; whereas many unbelievers were present at her memorial service, hearing about the certainty of eternal life for those who put their trust in Jesus Christ. I have since wondered about that in trying to understand the mystery of God's will and ways of working. But I certainly had no such thought at the time. As a family however we were deeply touched by the support of so many people. Some had travelled from as far away as Southampton or Bristol to be with us. Members of our church had laid on tea and cakes in the old church hall. We did not find the socialising easy as this was the first time we had had to cope with a crowd without Diana and of course most people wanted to come and speak to us. In the circumstances it was quite helpful that we had to leave before too long in order to get a meal for relatives needing to be on their way.

Reality set in once again the following day as I began to think about what might now constitute a 'normal' life. In some ways life was easier without the constant need to care for Diana but that in itself added to our aching void. I could actually feel the physical space which should have been occupied by Diana with my arms around her. It distressed me very much that I could do nothing at all about this emptiness or my longing to contain it. These feelings lasted off and on for nearly a year.

Christmas happened after a fashion although I don't recall too much about it. My parents came to stay. Christmas lunch was a painful experience. Before it had usually been a very happy time orchestrated by Diana. Finding myself to be the provider, cook, cleaner, present-buyer, card-writer and general keeper of the peace – in which role I failed badly most of the time, not being at peace myself – was a challenge which I only just survived much of the time. Sometimes I remembered to pray but I have to confess that at other times a few glasses of wine seemed more attractive and won out. My feelings tended to see-saw from neutral numbness to sheer disbelief that Diana was not coming back. For several months I would expect her to appear whenever a floorboard creaked or one of the cats or the dog pushed open a door. I also imagined she would be telephoning to say she was alive and nearby, although unable simply to turn up on the doorstep.

As well as or alternating with these feelings, I experienced anger towards God, anger and pity towards myself, envy and resentment towards couples, relief that Diana's suffering was finished and delight that she would be in heaven. Also, I could not understand why God should take a wonderful, witnessing and active Christian and allow a feeble specimen of Christianity such as myself to remain alive. But sometimes I had negative feelings about Diana – which seem incredible now but were real enough at the time. I couldn't avoid thinking of some of the less than happy moments in our marriage; times when we had been in conflict, usually over some insignificant matter which had been magnified out of all proportion. Thankfully there were not too many of these. But remembering them was a help in one respect. It is easy to think of one's dead spouse as having been perfect. It would have been particularly easy for me to go down that road, because Diana was such a lovely person, deservedly loved by many people who were all deeply upset at her death, and saying all kinds of good and perfectly true things about her. But remembering that she was in fact human and had one or two little faults was no bad thing, because it was part of the truth. Also, as far as I was concerned, it helped in a way to reduce the pain of her loss. Please don't misunderstand me: I am not suggesting that it is good to soften the blow by thinking badly of someone; merely that we should not fall into the trap of idolising him or her. My memory of Diana has been strengthened by remembering her real self, including the imperfect bits. As the months have passed I have been increasingly able to keep a picture of her and our relationship in its totality, warts and all, rather than projecting a painfully untrue image of perfection.

Our circle of friends includes both Christians and non-Christians and they have all been helpful in different ways, both in their attitude towards me and in their remembrance of Diana. I have always been invited to the social gatherings of non-Christian groups and have tried to go, even though it has felt very odd being there on my own. Now, twenty-eight months on, I am finding it easier. Even so, I don't like staying out late, because coming home on my own afterwards can still feel very empty, particularly, I find, after midnight. In the last six months I have started to have friends round for dinner, cooking simple meals from a 'thirty-minute' cookbook. The first few of these did seem strange without Diana, but I am now enjoying them and quite like cooking meals which are a bit different from the usual weekday food. I haven't invited more than one couple at a time as yet, not being sure that my culinary co-ordination could cope with the numbers involved!

Thankfully, there have been few occasions when people have said well-intentioned but hurtful things either at meals or other events. 'You must miss her a lot.' This is a natural remark but I find myself feeling anger as well as sadness if the tone in which it is said is just too casual. Some of my friends do have the ability to say just the right supportive things, but I am still sometimes surprised by my reaction, or lack of it, when comments are made about Diana. I find the occasional unpredictability of my emotions difficult, because for much of the time I can talk easily and happily about our life. Then, suddenly, I find myself getting emotional and needing to change the subject. But things are getting easier in this respect too as time goes on.

In 1996 I started to think about whether I could envisage the rest of life on my own. Before I met Diana I had thought that I would probably never get married so one might have expected that being on my own again wouldn't present too much of a problem. However, I realised that I do need all of the aspects of a close relationship and that I would want to remarry if I was to meet the right person. I prayed about the matter and left it in God's hands. Subsequently I have met a lady with whom I have developed a very strong relationship. We both want the same thing but are praying about the future and waiting for the Lord's response.

Family life in general has settled into a new pattern since Diana's death. Charlotte is settled at college so there are only two to cook and wash for most of the time. All the domestic activities are completed more or less on time and safely; we haven't had food poisoning or run out of loo rolls! It is sometimes a challenge coming home from work and having to set about cooking a meal and ironing a pile of shirts. Often while doing these things I feel lonely and miss Diana, not because I want her to do those chores but because I am reminded of how much she managed to do and of her continuing absence. Having plenty to do, however, means that I don't have too much time to feel sorry for myself; that I simply have to get on and cope. I think I am now more balanced in my perspective and emotions, and I'm able to remember Diana lovingly without feeling too sad. The anger I felt with God, myself, the doctor and Diana has gone and I feel much more of a whole person again. Many people were very supportive in prayer and, while I may not have known about it every time, I am sure that things would have been much worse had there not been so much prayer for the three of us.

I continue to read my Bible and pray. The notes I used after Diana's death were written by a man whose wife had also died of cancer after much prayer by many people. I found his comments helpful. I don't always keep up the discipline of personal daily reading and prayer; nor do I always feel helped when I do. But generally speaking, the more I make this a regular part of the pattern of my day and come with an open heart and mind to God, the more strength and light I receive.

I have thought about the fact that healing was not given to Diana and tried to rationalise it. I still believe that God does heal people today in the same way that he answers many other prayers, and that I have to try to trust in his greater purposes. We went through a testing time when so many people had been sure of healing only to see Diana getting worse. My basic faith was never challenged all through the period I have written about even though at times I was a very poor example of Christianity. I'd like to make one other comment about the healing question. It struck me at the time that if God wanted to heal Diana, he could have done it through prayer in our home quietly. I cannot feel that it is necessary to keep going somewhere, doing something, searching for hidden agendas, conjuring up more faith and the like. Indeed, sometimes doing those things can rob people of the rest and peace they may need; it can even give the impression that the healing comes from all our activities rather than from God.

The care and support of friends, both Christian, fringe believers and non-believers has meant that normality has been easier to accept and I have been able to feel comfortable, if not happy, about being on my own. I have now started to help with one of the young people's groups at our church. Initially I said I could not do this as I felt that I was not the right person. However, there seemed to be firm pressure coming from somewhere, so I accepted the work as something God wanted me to do. I am back in full swing at work, although I do leave early and make up by not having a lunch break. I do still miss Diana but have accepted the way things are without negative feelings and with a certain amount of optimism for the future. So it seems as though I am now as near to normal as I have ever been! It's tremendous to be able to say and feel that. When Diana died, I felt that life could never be good and I could never feel happy again. It was so hard to believe that I could change and heal. But to anyone reading this who has been recently bereaved, I now want to say, 'Please believe me – things *will* get better!'

Sheila's Story

Sheila Evans is a member of Rhiwbina Baptist Church, Cardiff, where she is a deacon responsible for women's ministry. She is the mother of three married children, Philip, Martyn and Rachel, and has nine grandchildren.

Sheila's story was written nine years after the death of her husband Ralph.

Sometimes when we have lost someone very close to us, we are ambivalent about coming through the bereavement. Do we really want to feel better? Would that not be a denial of the depth of love between us or disloyalty to the memory of the deceased? We feel similarly ambivalent about laughter and happy experiences; or when we suddenly realise that a whole day has gone by without our having even thought about our loss. Feelings of guilt are common in these situations and are part of the grieving process.

Sheila's Story

There is a stretch of wild rugged coastline in West Wales which is very special to me. All my childhood holidays were spent in that area and I have been back many times since. It took a whole day to get there on the train in those days, but when we did arrive we were transported into another world. There were several beaches along that coast. Some were sandy, others were better for swimming or offered vantage points to watch for seals. One beach however was different from the rest. It was a narrow inlet shaded by towering cliffs on each side, and our delight on that beach was to look for shells among all the pebbles. The shells we found were many and varied but in particular we used to search for the tiny, fragile, pink cowrie shell with its delicate markings. For hours we would sit, slowly sifting through the pebbles to look for these elusive shells. When our labours were rewarded the cry would go up in triumph, 'Found one!' and the rest would rush to the spot to look for more. Each one was so precious that it was carefully stored in a handkerchief until we got home. Sometimes we would go back to that beach after a violent storm and there amid the seaweed at high-water level we would find one or two cowrie shells intact, even after the tremendous battering of those relentless waves against the rocks. How we would marvel that the maelstrom which had tossed driftwood onto the beach and strewn great logs like matchsticks across the shore, had not harmed the tiny cowrie shell! It would still be intact, battered but not broken.

Sometimes storms in our lives build up over a long period of time. We see the dark clouds gathering on the horizon and then drawing nearer and nearer. For me, however, the storm in my life was sudden, dramatic, like the one whipped up on a summer's day as the disciples crossed the Sea of Galilee. They had set out in obedience to the command of Christ and yet half way across it looked as though they would be engulfed by the waves. Their very existence was threatened.

It had started off a perfectly normal Tuesday morning. My daughter had returned to her work in Carmarthen, and my husband Ralph had left for work in the Cardiff Royal Infirmary where he was a consultant paediatrician. I had taken my bowl of coleslaw to our church coffee shop in the village. I then returned home to await our mother and toddler group which would be arriving shortly for their weekly Bible study. As I waited, the phone rang – and my life has never been the same since that moment in time. My hopes and dreams for the future lay shattered at my feet. I found myself in the middle of the biggest storm of my life. But, like that cowrie shell on the beach, I was to experience the Lord keeping me safe in the deep waters and bringing me through into the sunshine once more.

My husband, with no previous history of heart disease, had suffered a massive heart attack while driving the car to hospital. By the time one of his colleagues had rung me, it was too late. I had had no time to say goodbye. I used to regret that so much at first, but then eventually realised that even if death comes after a prolonged illness, people still feel that they have not adequately said goodbye. No way were we prepared for the tearing apart of a strong loving marriage of twenty-nine years. My farewell was the customary kiss as he left for work that morning and the assurance that there was nothing spoiling our relationship.

At the infirmary I was taken to a small room off the casualty area. My son Martyn and his wife Julie who worked close by were already there. So too was the professor of paediatrics and several other consultants. All were devastated. One by one they offered their most sincere and obviously heartfelt sympathy before moving out of the stunned silence back to the bustle of a busy hospital. Two remained behind – Professor Gray and Dr Weaver, two wonderful Christian friends in the department. Quietly but firmly they took me to see the now lifeless body. I am so grateful to them for that. I was too numb even to cry. My mind was in a whirl, and I was filled with a sense of total inadequacy, but seeing the body was the first tiny step towards grasping the reality of death – something my stunned brain couldn't or wouldn't take in at first.

Some days later on one of his visits, our GP, who was a friend of Ralph's from student days, asked what effect my husband's death had had on my faith. As I thought about that question, in all honesty I could say to him that although completely devastated by what had happened, I could see many glimpses of the goodness of the Lord, like shafts of light piercing the gloom. I was prepared to trust God even though I did not understand.

One blessing was the kindness and care shown by the staff of the infirmary and by Ralph's colleagues in the Children's Centre at the University Hospital of Wales. They too were grieving and helped me so much in my grief, and the contact has continued through the ensuing years.

A further shaft of light came when another medical friend called. He told me that he had been driving behind Ralph's car when it had swerved to the side and crashed into a lamp-post near a bus-stop. Quickly pulling up and going to investigate, he had soon been shocked to realise that Ralph was the person crumpled over the steering wheel, not able to answer to his name. Amazingly, an ambulance had actually been coming down the road at that moment, so when Ralph had been transferred to this, our friend had gone with him. He went on to assure me that my husband had not suffered. No time had been lost in getting him to the hospital, resuscitation had been attempted immediately and every possible effort had been made to save him. How good of the Lord to encourage me with that glimpse of his divine plan!

Some time later when my son was driving along that same part of the road, he noticed several mothers and children waiting at the bus-stop. How we thanked the Lord that a man who had devoted his life to helping children had not been responsible for harming any in his death!

These and other incidents helped me to understand that God's timing is perfect. Someone has said that written across the shield of faith should be the words 'God makes no mistakes' or 'Man is immortal until his work is done'. I could only conclude that, sad as we were, Ralph's work was done here in this life and he was now with his Lord whom he loved so dearly.

After a most moving thanksgiving service for his life led with great sensitivity by David Juliff, our pastor, and Professor Peter Gray, we went on to the crematorium. It was a dark wet November day but as we sang the last verse of 'Love Divine' and came to the words 'Changed from glory into glory till in heaven we take our place', the wintry sun broke through the clouds and a shaft of light played on the coffin just before the curtains moved inexorably across. I have never been more sure of the after-life than at that moment. Some find great solace in a gravestone or memorial. I respect that. But what I knew then was that I could say with the angel of old, 'He is not here, he is risen.'

The funeral service was held in a neighbouring Baptist church as our own was undergoing extensive enlargement at the time. The place was packed with family, friends and colleagues from over the years and many more stood in the rain outside. There was barely room for us to walk to the front, and that packed church has always remained as my abiding image of the love and support showered on us as a family by so many dear friends from all walks of life. How we valued them and their prayer support! We knew a peace that passed understanding and a strength that was not of ourselves. I believe we should never underestimate the power of prayer and of the comforter who can take us past breaking point while keeping us from breaking. Daily the postman brought hundreds of letters of sympathy and love. To read them I had to settle down with a large box of tissues at my side. Some were from people in important positions, others from friends recalling happy memories of Ralph. Some of the most moving were from parents of handicapped children whom my husband had helped. All were very precious. I was only sorry that Ralph could not see them too.

Words are inadequate to express how much my family has meant to me in this situation. I always remember them coming in one by one on that fateful day. Martyn and Julie were already with me. Rachel came back from Carmarthen and her husband from Oslo where he was on business. My eldest son Philip and his wife came from Exeter with their small baby. As they stopped at a service station to feed him, Philip overheard a man saying on the phone, 'I'm coming home to see you, Dad,' and he was suddenly struck by the devastating thought that he would never be able to say those words again. All were grieving in their own way. Thankfully, as they had all had a strong relationship with their father, their grief was not compounded by the guilt of unfinished business. What had happened had highlighted for us all the need to keep open healthy relationships, for who knows what a day will bring?

Philip and Martyn saw to the medical and legal side of affairs while they all worked together on the 101 things to be done at home. Ralph's pyjamas and slippers were quietly removed before I went to bed that night. I was plied with endless cups of tea and coffee and even protected from the overwhelming number of visitors and phone calls. Church friends brought us so many cakes to eat that we were quite spoiled for choice! Another young friend cleared Ralph's belongings from the car and was intrigued to find, alongside his AA map, his Bible – his very real guide to life. Our pastor's wife took me to their home one afternoon. It was lovely to go out but I still remember the shock of realising that life in the outside world was going on as usual even though my world had fallen apart. While I was out, the men went to Cardiff Arms Park and their wives watched a video. We cried a lot but we laughed a lot as well. We also spoke of Ralph together and that was very therapeutic. There was so much to thank God for that week. What a privilege to have family and friends with whom we are safe to cry, laugh and pray!

The thanksgiving service proved to be a tremendous experience. We had all been dreading, in a way, this huge ordeal ahead, but again the Lord brought us through. When the last visitor had left our home that day, we drew the curtains and the seven of us settled down with a grateful sigh of relief. My relief was short-lived. Philip said, 'Now that was the easy part over, Mum.' It took a while to grasp the full impact of his words but the long days, weeks and months ahead were to prove their wisdom. After the service and all the busyness, the long process of healing and readjustment began.

The most immediate problem was learning to live on my own. Over and over again I asked myself, 'Will I ever get used to this?' The nights were long and sometimes sleep eluded me. I learnt not to count sheep but to talk to the shepherd who was always with me. I became in a very real sense far more dependent on him as my refuge and protection. Like so many who live on their own, I found that going away was good, but then, of course, I had to come back to an empty house knowing there was no one there with whom I could talk over the experience. On returning home after visiting, shopping or anything else, my heartache would intensify as the key went in the door, and I realised afresh that there would be no one with whom I could share the excitement of seeing a new item bought on a shopping trip, or discuss the latest family news.

The practical details of looking after the house, the garden and the car I found difficult as well. So many of these·areas had been Ralph's responsibility so as I at first grappled with the ever-growing trees or tried to cope with the vagaries of flat roofs, I would say, 'Ralph, why have you left me to see to this on my own?' It was then that, time and time again, family and friends came to my rescue in such practical ways. They were all so patient and I valued their love and help. I felt like a gangling fawn, learning to walk. I stumbled my way through that first year.

Although the house had its problems, it was a tremendous place of security too. Sometimes when out with friends I would have this overwhelming desire to go back home. The sheer business of socialising was such an effort at times that I just needed to escape. I am thankful for friends who understood this and allowed me to be myself.

The grieving process goes on for a very long time especially where, as with Ralph and myself, the love has been very deep and the lives of the couple very closely intertwined. So often people expect you to be over it in a few short weeks or months. I found that if I wore my red winter coat and put on a big smile, people thought I was all right. They never knew that as I drove the car I needed wipers on my eyes not on the windscreen. Many encouraged me to think that after the first year was over, when one had been through all the anniversaries, birthdays and other memorable dates, everything would be so much better. I woke on 4th November the following year and felt exactly the same. I was still hurting! In Victorian days when a widow wore her weeds for two years, all could read the signal that she was still grieving. While in no way advocating mourning in that sense, I think that perhaps we as a society need to be more sensitive to those who are suffering in this way.

All this and so much more was part of learning to walk alone. C. S. Lewis in his book *A Grief Observed* talks about losing a partner being like an amputation. The person learns to live with one leg and to adapt to a new way of life with an artificial leg, but whenever she gets up in the morning, or takes a bath or shower, she is made all too painfully aware that part of her is missing. As with anything, the more one does it, the easier it becomes until eventually one does it without thinking. I can still remember the agony of my first visit to the post office to draw my widow's pension, but very quickly that became part of the routine of my new way of life and was done without thinking.

More of a problem in fact lay in the designation 'widow'. Some time after Ralph's death, I went on a course at which we were asked to introduce ourselves and say something about our situation, family, work and so on. I found that I could not bring myself to say, 'I am a widow.' I did, however, feel more at ease with the term by the end of the week's course. In the opening chapter of *Alone*, a book by Katie Wiebe, the author speaks of how she tells a group of widows gathered around that they will not always be 'widows'. She wasn't suggesting necessarily that they would marry, but rather that the pain and even the denigration implicit in that word would gradually recede as their own identity re-emerged and even blossomed. Through the very changing seasons of life, one might be single, married, widowed and then single again. Widowhood is a painful state through which one can pass and from which one can emerge into a different life of service to the Lord: a life in which one is no longer living *in* the past while carrying *from* it many precious memories; a life in which faith has been deepened by having walked through the valley and found light at the end of the tunnel.

One of the other difficult things for me was making my heart catch up with my head. Many verses which well-meaning Christians shared with me caused me much heart-searching. Yes, I knew what the Scripture was saying, but I did not – for example – want God to be my husband! I wanted human love, as I had known it in a deep marriage relationship – 'love with skin on it', as someone once said. Others were quick to point out that 'all things work together for good to those who love God' (Romans 8:28). I did believe that with my head but my heart had a long way to go to catch up with such thinking. Sometimes it was the words of hymns which caused me problems, particularly some of the Easter hymns. I could joyfully affirm the truth of the resurrection, and yet death still had a sting in its tail – simply the very human pain of separation and loss.

Sometimes when we have lost someone very close to us, we are ambivalent about coming through the bereavement. Do we really want to feel better? Would that not be a denial of the depth of love between us or disloyalty to the memory of the deceased? We feel similarly ambivalent about laughter and happy experiences, or when we suddenly realise that a whole day has gone by without our having even thought about our loss. Feelings of guilt are common in these situations and are part of the grieving process. A mother who lost her young son in the Dunblane tragedy found later on that she was pregnant again. She said that one part of her reacted with joy to the news but another was overwhelmed by something close to guilt. She felt disloyal to the memory of her son and his unique position in their family. Only when she realised how thrilled he would have been to have had new twins in the family did she start to come to terms with the pregnancy. When the Lord in his infinite patience continues to ask, 'What do you want me to do for you?' we often struggle to say, 'Yes, Lord, I do want to be healed.'

In addition to being willing to recover and feel better and happier, we may need to deal with bitterness, refusing to harbour such feelings. Reverend Stanley Voke preaching in Rhiwbina soon after Ralph died, took me to one side at the end of the service and said, 'Keep the wound clean.' It is easy to become bitter or full of self-pity or even envious of other couples strolling hand in hand on a summer's evening or doing things which you and your spouse used to do as a couple but now no longer can. 'Why me?' can be a destructive question and foster a 'root of bitterness' which damages the person in whom it is growing. Acceptance of the situation is a vital key to healing, and to preventing the wound from becoming like a gnawing ulcer, liable to keep opening up and getting infected.

Along with trying to deal with such matters, I also found that I needed to search for my own identity. So much of my life outside the family had been tied up with Ralph's position and role, both as a paediatrician in the local teaching hospital and as an elder in our church. Even when I was speaking at women's meetings I had often been introduced as Ralph's wife. After his death – I was just me! I had lost my security, my self-image was at its lowest point and I had no designated role behind which I could hide. But it was at this point, when I was in the depths, that the truths which I had learnt in happier times started to become real to me. My security was in Christ, not in any human person, however close. By his grace, my greatest needs had been met. His love for me was unconditional and he accepted me as I was. However I felt, I was precious in his sight. Very gently, through his word and through the unwavering love and support of the church, the Lord reaffirmed these truths to me.

My journey through the valley has in many ways reminded me of my days in university when I first became a Christian. There I came to a point where I admitted my need, believed in the finished work of Christ and accepted salvation by his grace. Now, too, I have had to be realistic about my situation and my own inadequacy, come to the 'wounded healer' and accept the healing which he offers and his firm promise of hope, not just for that grand reunion in eternity but for life today and tomorrow. When we returned from hospital on the day Ralph died, I remember musing aloud, 'Where do I go from here?' Julie, one of my daughters-in-laws, replied, 'There is only one way to go – forward, of course.' As the prospect of years on my own stretched endlessly before me, I felt completely daunted. But I had to learn to take one day at a time and to trust God for the future. Like many others I have found that perhaps, contrary to expectations, time by itself does not always heal, but it does distance one from the trauma. To put it another way, the hole remains, but I can identify with Ingrid Trobisch when she describes how the Lord enabled her to build a bridge over the hole from which she could reach out to others.

The Lord has helped me to build this bridge mainly through my own church but also through opportunities to share experiences with other Christians. In Rhiwbina Baptist Church I became a deacon involved with women's ministry and also a member of the pastoral care team. Although my family are all away from Cardiff now, the Lord has provided a very special church family here and I continue to thank him for such love and care and find it a privilege to have opportunities to serve them now in his name.

Three years before Ralph died, the Lord led us as a church to open a coffee shop and bookshop in the heart of Rhiwbina. It was a very exciting venture and a step of faith in obedience to what we felt was God's very clear guidance. The whole church caught the vision of a meeting place where the love of God would reach out into the com-

munity attracting people of whom many would never
cross the threshold of the church. The word of God and
Christian literature were now available on the main street.
Next to the butcher's shop and opposite the bread shop, we
were offering the bread of life! Many from the church were
involved in the shop – serving, cooking, preparing, cleaning or seeing to the finances, while I myself had been
responsible in a small way for setting up the bookshop. It
was exciting to see the Lord supply our needs and bless the
venture far beyond the limits of our feeble faith.

The shop was called 'The Olive Branch' because we saw
it as a place of peace, healing and refreshment in the widest
sense. Now I was to experience these things for myself
there. Here was a place to which I could go at any time and
meet friends who understood and cared and would sit
down for a welcome cup of coffee with me. Also, serving
in the bookshop a couple of times a week brought me into
contact with Christians from other churches in the Cardiff
area and with friends from the neighbourhood. The Olive
Branch has seen many changes since those early days but
its goals remain the same as it continues to be a beacon in
the shopping heart of the village. I thank God for it.

Soon after setting up The Olive Branch, and once we had
larger premises for our church, we were led to set up our
own nursery school. As Ralph was so involved with children in a professional capacity, this vision was close to his
heart. As with The Olive Branch, so here too the Lord called
just the right person to lead that work. She was a head
teacher who gave up a full-time career to set up and run the
nursery school. This too has had a big impact on young
families in the district. For these last six years it has been
my privilege to chair the management committee and so be
involved with the staff as they seek to share the love of the
Lord, not only with the children but also with their families.

Being involved in so much was a tremendous blessing to

me: activities like these became focal points in weeks which would otherwise have seemed shapeless. Slowly but surely the green shoots of recovery appeared like snow-drops in the winter sunshine, emerging from the hard barren ground, braving frost, wind and rain, and bringing with them the promise of spring. God is faithful and so patient. He has taken me very gently step by step along the way – always being there, always encouraging, supporting and strengthening but never driving me beyond my limits. At last I began to see the truth in Isaiah's words, 'Your days of sorrow will end.'

In ancient Palestine, people in mourning would tear their clothes and wear sackcloth and ashes. The mourners would also take off their sandals and walk barefoot. Moses and Joshua were both commanded to take off their shoes in the presence of the Lord. Later on the children of Israel were instructed to eat the Passover meal in a state of readi-ness to move when the time was right. Their cloaks were to be tucked into their belts, their sandals were to be on their feet and their staffs in their hands. They were to be ready for action, for whatever the future might hold. There came a time for me, too, to put on my shoes, as it were, and to face the future, no longer as a 'widow' but as 'Sheila' – a person, secure in the love of the almighty Father, and ready to be obedient to his ever-unfolding plan.

So by his grace and through the tremendous love of my family and friends, this cowrie shell is still intact. It has come through the buffeting of the waves and storms and is hopefully more translucent than before. A different pattern has been etched by the maker on the shell – a pattern for eternity. As this shell is held up to the light I humbly pray that the light of Jesus might shine through, giving glory back to him.

Elsie's Story

Elsie Harris now lives in Nottingham. Formerly, she and her husband were medical missionaries with the Leprosy Mission and worked in India, Nepal and Zaire. She is the mother of two married children and has five grandchildren.

Elsie's story was written nearly two years after the death of her husband John.

As I approach the second anniversary of John's death, I miss him as much as ever. In our spiritual partnership he was always the teacher, someone with a tremendous love for God's word, which he wanted to share with me. But I can rejoice because I know, as one of my grandchildren said, 'He is having such a lovely time in heaven.'

I am still very vulnerable. Something which happened recently brought this home to me. I was shopping in town when suddenly, just in front of me, was someone wearing a sports coat similar to the one John had. Instinctively, I reached out to the man, before realising my mistake and hastily withdrawing my hand. Then the tears came.

Elsie's Story

'Elsie's kite has flown away.' So said a missionary colleague and friend on hearing the news of the sudden 'homecall' to heaven of my beloved husband John. She saw us, the Harris partnership, as being rather like a kite. John was the actual kite and I was the string attached to it, and both of us were being 'flown' by God, who was holding the string and in control. The kite often flew high but sometimes the string tried to pull it down a bit. In the same way, perhaps, John and I helped to balance one another as we united in serving God.

As I write this, I realise how privileged we were in our thirty-nine years together. There were times when we experienced 'ditching' in various valleys along our route, but always we were held in God's strong hand which was more than capable of getting us airborne again each time. That was the pattern until 9th March 1995. On that day, the kite was suddenly severed from its string and entered God's presence. John, the kite, had been so ready for that. But what about me, the string? I was left behind, in a crumpled heap, unable to fly as before because no longer attached to the kite. But I was still held securely in God's strong hand. He had promised, 'I will never leave you nor forsake you.'

Wednesday 8th March had begun much like any other day in our lives at that time in Zaire. I remember hearing

John singing happy birthday to his sister Doreen so I knew his thoughts and prayers were with her on her special day. In the morning he was busy in the office, working on statistics – an aspect of leprosy work which he liked the least but knew to be necessary. He preferred to be out and about alongside his patients and students. At seventy years of age, he was fit and able. Although officially retired from the mission, he had wanted to stay in Zaire where he felt his remaining strength and experience could be used.

Usually on a Wednesday I would drive myself and others in the landrover to a women's prayer meeting. But on that day John wanted to go the hangar to leave a new car battery with Will, the mechanic. So he said he would drive and drop us off. We piled into the large vehicle – about four women and the same number of children. I sat in the front with John and between us was Alyssa aged four. She put her hands on the wheel, pretending to help John drive, while he chatted happily with her.

We arrived at the house where we were going to pray and everyone got out except John, who said he would be back to pick us up at about four o'clock in the afternoon. Then he drove away.

I had only been in the house about twenty minutes when Will, the mechanic, turned up, his unexpected arrival being the first indication that something was amiss. He said, 'Elsie, please come quickly – there's been an accident and John's been hurt.' 'Badly?' I asked, but Will's expression was blank as he replied, 'I don't know how badly.'

Within minutes I was at the hospital at John's side. He was in pain and bleeding but he held my hand and said, 'Elsie.' I urged him not to try to speak. Later, I went with him to the X-ray department but the staff there had trouble getting adequate X-rays of his broken jaw. I waited outside the department with another doctor's wife, whose presence was a comfort to me. I was concerned about John's jaw but pleased that he was conscious and able to talk, having as yet no inkling of any other injuries. After a while he was taken to the operating room and I was advised to go home.

Later, the dentist who had done the operation came to tell me that he had wired John's jaw. But he added that John would soon need to go to Nairobi to have plates inserted. After hearing that, I went straight back to the hospital. As I ran down the hill, my head was full of plans for taking care of John and in particular helping him to eat. It didn't occur to me that I would have much more serious things to face.

I arrived at the hospital expecting to see John but instead I was told that he hadn't come round from the anaesthetic. So I sat outside the operating room, on my own, waiting for what seemed a very long time. I thought of others who had sat and waited as I was doing and identified with what they would have been feeling.

Eventually a young German doctor came out and very gently explained to me that John's vital signs had given cause for concern but that he was now stable though still unconscious. He suggested that I should stay where I was, promising that he wouldn't leave John until he had come round. My nursing training alerted me to the possibility of John's being brain-damaged. Even so, in the midst of my desolation, I experienced an amazing sense of peace.

Suddenly the operating room door opened and John, still unconscious, was brought out on a trolley. I walked along beside him as he was wheeled into a side room. On the way, he managed to squeeze my hand. Friends came to be with me as I watched at his bedside. Even some of the young mothers who were there with their children were anxious to help. A rota was organised so that someone would always be with me. That night a British nurse insisted on staying with John so that I could get some rest.

Early next morning, I could see that John was unable to respond to me in any way. Our friends came and went throughout the day. Quietly, graciously, they stayed with me and prayed with me. That evening, John slipped quietly into God's presence.

After the funeral service on 10th March, I wrote to tell family and friends what had happened.

Loving greetings from Zaire. Just a week ago, John and I were together rejoicing in all God's goodness to us. Today he is safely at home with the Lord. On Wednesday, he was in the landrover approaching the Missionary Aviation Fellowship hangar when a steel pipe sprang up and rammed through the dashboard. It hit his head and face. He was rushed to hospital, following this bizarre accident. He was bleeding a lot, had a broken jaw and collar bone and other wounds. At that time he was conscious and tried to speak. One of the doctors gave blood and the dentist operated to wire his jaw. After that he did not speak again, but was able at first to communicate through a hand squeeze. He slipped away peacefully at 7.30 pm on 9th March while I was close by him. The love and concern shown by nationalists and expatriates was simply amazing. 'The love of Jesus, what it is, none but his loved ones know.'

Later that evening John's body was taken to the hospital chapel where a large crowd had gathered, including church leaders and the local chief. Next morning he was taken to the Nyankunde Church with trumpeters leading the procession and the nursing school students walking behind the coffin. The church was packed to capacity with friends from nearby stations representing different missions in this part of Zaire and joining us for the service of thanksgiving for his life and testimony here. A radio message was read out from Nebobongo where the entire station had gathered for a similar time of worship and thanksgiving. Beautiful wreaths of tropical flowers from local gardens were made by the women and girls. All the funeral arrangements were carried out by our many African friends. After the church service the long procession made the journey to the local grave site. At the grave there was more singing and more tributes and the finale was the Hallelujah Chorus played by the trumpeters.

John was a man greatly loved. We sorrowed in our human loss of him but the note of triumph was predominant as we

thought of him being 'absent from the body but present with
the Lord'. He was laid in a beautiful spot alongside the airstrip,
among the people he had loved and served. Before the funeral,
I read: 'The Lord is my strength and shield; my heart trusts in
him and I am helped, therefore my heart greatly rejoices, and
with my song will I praise him.'

As I experienced the numbness of grief, with the knowledge that life neither would nor could be the same again,
I also knew the reality of being loved – by the Christians in
Zaire and also, as soon as they heard what had happened,
by Christians in Britain. I thought of others in their shock
and grief: of my son and daughter and other family
members who hadn't been able to attend the funeral
service. That must have been very hard for them but God
provided me with someone to help me at that time: Rob, a
young man who had come as a short-term worker with
Tear Fund and who, we discovered, was a distant relation
of John's. In those early hours and days, he quietly helped
me in what had been our home on the hill but was now
empty of John's presence. Along with the young German
doctor, Rob also supported me during the funeral.

As the first numbness wore off, I felt the pain, very
intensely at times, as the reality of my loss hit me. One day
I walked into the office and pulled out some paper, and out
fell one of the poems John used to write for me from time
to time. This one urged me to keep going on steadily and
sacrificially in my Christian life and work, and was signed
'ever your loving John'. This, I felt, was a command to obey
– something I needed to do, rather than withdrawing and
hiding, which would have been a tempting alternative in
my grief.

Of course, I shed many tears in those days, especially
when I was alone, but also when I was with certain very
understanding people. Such tears were healing, and I
thank God for the supportive friends he gave me then and
in Cornerstone Evangelical Church in Nottingham later on.

Grieving, I have found, is an ongoing necessary process. But I believe it needs to be given to God and shared with him, as well as with others, rather than being hugged to oneself.

Even before John's death I had had to learn to live alone with the Lord. When John went on safaris in order to reach leprosy patients or students, I sometimes accompanied him but often stayed and looked after the office. The only good part of such separations were the reunions. John enjoyed writing poems and would slip one beneath my pillow before leaving me for one of his trips. Whatever passage of Scripture he was meditating on at the time would form the content of his poems which he would write out on pretty, recycled cards.

When it was time for John to return, I would be at the airstrip to watch his little plane land and then to see him hop out and run straight into my arms. He always had a kind of radiance about him and was bubbling with things he wanted to share. One thing that fostered our closeness as a couple was that we read the same Bible passages even when we were apart.

Now there would be no new poems. But what a wealth of 'old' ones I still had, which I could read and reread. They evoke very precious memories. And they speak of the reunion awaiting us: a reunion with each other and with God. That is my joy and hope.

Ten days after John's funeral a number of African women gathered at the house on the hill for a meeting. We had a wonderful time of singing and sharing. When asked to speak, I said that I believed John was like Enoch who had walked and talked with God and been ready to go 'home' to him. After the meeting had broken up and everyone had slipped quietly away, I noticed the gifts which people had left for me: eggs, rice, sugar, soap, pineapples. They had given these things to me out of their poverty and I found such generosity very poignant and precious.

The weeks and months which followed were very busy ones for me, as I got ready to hand over the work to our successors. John had very few possessions but I thought and prayed hard before giving away each item. During this time, I was very well cared for by missionary colleagues: meals in their homes and the love of their children brought me much comfort. Letters and cards began to pour in from around the world. I was amazed and pleased by what people wrote as they remembered John and spoke of what he meant to them. A special joy was to have my daughter Lois with me for a few days in Kenya. We walked back and forth along the beach in Mombasa, sharing our grief, but also encouraged in the knowledge that many people were praying for us.

John often said the Psalms expressed every aspect of our changing life and should be used to help us pour out our hearts to God. I followed this suggestion and found it to be helpful.

I remember other things John said, particularly during our last months together. At the end of 1994 he remarked one day, 'I wonder what the Lord has for us in 1995, as it's the first time in ten years I have not got any candidates listed for a teaching course.' The reason for the lack of students was the difficult political situation which made travelling a problem. Soon after making that remark, John received an unexpected invitation. It was to give a key-note address in Malaysia in January 1995 at a conference for further medical education for missionary doctors and dentists in Asia. John badly wanted me to accompany him and now I am so glad that I did. Quite apart from being with John, I enjoyed the fellowship and attended some very interesting lectures. John's message was Psalm 18 – a psalm that was very precious to him.

On our return journey via Singapore, we celebrated our thirty-ninth wedding anniversary. We went to the Botanical Gardens where we saw, among other things, many beautiful varieties of orchids. We were accompanied by a Norwegian dentist and his wife who had also been at the conference. They invited us to their hotel for dinner. We very much enjoyed the meal and our time of prayer with them afterwards.

Very early the next morning, John sprang a surprise on me. 'We're having breakfast in a park with the birds today,' he said, beaming. After a long taxi ride we reached the park. The colourful macaws put on a splendid performance for their visitors. Then we went shopping and John bought me a lovely watch. The next day, which was Sunday, we worshipped with Singaporean friends in the basement of the Garden Hotel. A visiting singing group took part in the morning service. Remembering the conviction with which they sang a song about nothing being too difficult for God, I have often felt reassured and comforted.

On arrival at the guest house in Nairobi, we met Peg and Les Green, a missionary couple from America who had come out to hold a seminar for Christians from the pygmy people. They invited us to join them for four days of preaching and teaching in the forest. Les met us at the airstrip in a tractor and we climbed in, as did also a large number of pygmy people who had come out to welcome us. We all sang as we proceeded to bump along.

After lunch we went out to the forest in an all-terrain vehicle with huge wheels. It proved an exciting ride as we went through streams and over fallen branches. The pygmies had prepared a clearing in the forest and were busy making igloo-shaped shelters using sticks and leaves. The one they made for us was big enough for the Greens to sleep at one end and John and me at the other. When the local chief arrived at the scene to find out what was happening, the pygmies simply extended our hut to accommodate him as well.

The roof was so low that we could only stand upright in the doorway. Bamboo beds had been made for us and these were attached to the forest floor. How John laughed at me rolling into my bed-bag at night and out of it in the morning – as I did at him performing the same feat! A wood fire which was kept burning all night outside the huts kept wild animals at bay.

We held meetings morning and evening. The pygmies either sat on the ground or on fallen tree trunks. John spoke a great deal about heaven, asking his hearers, 'Will I meet you there?'

In our role as medics, we went from hut to hut during the day looking for early signs of leprosy, but found none. Instead we found plenty of sick babies to treat. There were also people with nasty infected wounds, some of which needed soaking before treatment. The patients used their hoes to dig holes in the forest floor which they then lined with some of the enormous waterpoof forest leaves which could be put to many other uses, such as cooking pot lids, umbrellas or carrier bags. Once lined, the holes were ready to receive a mixture of water and antiseptic. After the patients had soaked their wounds in this, we were able to attend to them.

The pygmy men went hunting each day and brought back whatever they managed to catch and kill, such as monkey, deer or wild pig. They used forest twine to make their string hunting nets, which they would repair in the evenings. Peg Green gave some reading lessons in Swahili to a few men and distributed needles and thread or razor blades as prizes. At night we all sat outside with starlight overhead and firelight all around us.

On our return to Nyankunde, John was asked to help a man, not a leprosy patient, who was in danger of losing his foot altogether through gross ulceration. Due to a birth defect, his foot was twisted. After careful thought and preparation, John decided to operate. The foot was corrected and eventually, after much physiotherapy, the man was able to walk again normally.

Another patient was a young pilot's wife who had a large non-malignant wart near her mouth. John took great care to remove this without leaving a scar. After John's death, the pilot came and talked with me. He said he had been planning to give up flying for Missionary Aviation in Zaire because the pressures had become too great for him and because he had lost his first love for Jesus. Then he added, 'Elsie, I want you to know that I have rededicated my life to the Lord because I saw him so at work in John's life.'

Those are just some of the happy memories I have of our life together. Married in Africa in 1956, we had moved many times in the course of our leprosy work in Africa, India and Nepal, living in 'Heinz 57' varieties of accommodation. The bungalow on the hill became a very special home and base for our work in Zaire. Well constructed by an American missionary builder, it had a galvanised roof and cement floors, and was very adequate for our home and office needs. We moved in before the work was completed and I remember John laughingly carrying me to the front door over an area of rubble which was later to become a verandah. While waiting for the house to be built, we had been getting simple furniture made from local materials in readiness for our new home. Afterwards, when everything was finished and in place, we felt that all the waiting had been worth it.

Leaving the bungalow and facing all the adjustments of returning to life in Britain was almost a second bereavement for me. I wondered how I would manage it all. The answer was to take one day at a time with Jesus. There seemed to be an awful lot of hurdles for me to jump over. But in God's strength and power and with much prayer backing, I jumped them one at a time.

Ten days before my leaving date, my daughter and her husband and three children came out to Zaire. David, my son, came a week later. My family helped to landscape

John's grave and to erect a simple but lovely headstone. Our grandchildren planted zephrantes or storm-lilies: small, crocus-like pink flowers which need very little care and which open up after storms. The family mingled happily with my African friends and having them with me was a great help when the time came for me to lock the door of the home which John and I had shared for fourteen years, and to hand over the key.

Adjusting to life in Britain was eased by the love of my children and the spontaneous hugs of my grandchildren; also by the love of our extended families and the thoughtfulness of many friends. For some months I lived with members of the family but later the right place was found for me and my prayer is that God will use it for blessing.

As I approach the second anniversary of John's death, I miss him as much as ever. In our spiritual partnership he was always the teacher, someone with a tremendous love for God's word, which he wanted to share with me. But I can rejoice because I know, as one of my grandchildren said, 'He is having such a lovely time in heaven.'

I am still very vulnerable. Something which happened recently brought this home to me. I was shopping in town when suddenly, just in front of me, was someone wearing a sports coat similar to the one John had. Instinctively, I reached out to the man, before realising my mistake and hastily withdrawing my hand. Then the tears came.

Thinking of John's sports coat reminds me of how John disliked buying anything for himself. His previous coat had been worn for years; our son David joked about Harris tweed going on and on. When John eventually decided to replace it with a new garment, he set about it in his usual style – at the double: racing into the shop, flicking through the selection available, choosing a jacket, trying it on for size, deciding it was fine, going to the counter to pay for it, and finally rushing out, leaving the salesman, Lois and myself gasping!

After John's death, I gave this, John's last coat, to Gideon, an elder in the church who had been unwell for some time. John had often sat by his bedside to comfort and pray with him. Once Gideon had had a distressing attack of hiccups and John had filled a thermos flask with small pieces of ice for him to suck and so gain some relief. After John's death, Gideon struggled up the hill in order to pray with me. With tears streaming down his face, he said, 'He has raced me to heaven.'

God had often spoken to John and me through rainbows. I remember a beautiful one spanning the Nyankunde valley after John's death. A verse from the hymn by George Matheson refers to a rainbow and echoes what I feel:

> O Joy that seekest me through pain,
> I cannot close my heart to thee;
> I trace the rainbow through the rain
> And feel the promise is not vain
> That morn shall tearless be.

Jana's Story

Jana Godfrey is an American who has been living in England for almost thirteen years. She married her English scientist husband in 1984 and they settled in Oxford. A little over a year later, Phil was diagnosed as HIV positive, having been infected from the blood products he was given for his haemophilia. The couple had a daughter, Natasha, but while she was still very young, Phil died, aged thirty-four.

Jana's story, for this book, was written five and half years after the death of her husband. Her story *The Last Mountain – Living With AIDS* was published by Hodder and Stoughton in 1993.

As time passed, the awfulness of Phil's death began to fade slightly from my memory and I began to miss him more. I missed his hugs and his touch. I missed his sense of humour. I missed his help with household jobs. From time to time I felt sorry for myself – I had to do everything: paying the bills, carrying out the rubbish, taking the car to the garage. I also missed the emotional support that he had given so freely.

Jana's Story

When I married Phil in 1984, I knew that he suffered from haemophilia and depended on human blood products in order to live. His haemophilia, which had weakened his joints and sometimes caused him to walk with a limp, had made me ask myself: Will I be able to cope if he has to use a wheelchair? I knew I would.

At the time of our wedding, I had no idea what AIDS was. Even when one of my best friends, upon hearing that Phil was a haemophiliac, asked me, 'Aren't you scared of AIDS?' I blithely responded, 'No,' although I hadn't a clue what she was talking about. I was in love and fully expected to be celebrating a fiftieth wedding anniversary in the far-off future.

The eldest of four sisters, I grew up in New York State. Once I had finished university and had begun my working life in the travel industry, I decided I had had enough of the harsh upstate winters and moved to the warmer climate of Virginia. I found a job in Richmond and began my new life, 500 miles away from my family and friends. Part of building a new life in a new place was finding a church. I chose First Baptist Church of Richmond, as I had grown up attending a Baptist church. My new church family consisted of some 4,000 members but I soon felt at home.

I first met Phil in the context of the young singles Sunday school class. He was working in the States for two years as a post-doctoral research scientist. I was initially attracted by his English accent; his scruffiness, on the other hand, took a bit of getting used to. We became friends as we shared journeys to various church and social activities. I enjoyed hearing Phil's stories about England and we shared common ground in our love of the cinema. Some ten months later I knew I was in love and wanted to spend the rest of my life with him. I had always wondered how you knew when the 'right' person came along. Friends who had already settled into married life told me, 'You just know' – not a very satisfactory explanation. Now, suddenly I *did* know.

However, Phil took a bit of convincing. He told me he wasn't sure what love was. In spite of his protests, I knew he cared for me. I wasn't about to let him return to England without making my feelings known. So I took my courage in both hands, introduced the subject of marriage and told him that if he asked me to marry him, I'd say 'yes'. Phil worried that I'd be unhappy living in a different country if he were unable to find a permanent job in the States and had to return to England. He also felt that his haemophilia made his future prospects somewhat uncertain although the treatment that had become available meant he was likely to have a normal life span. Although we casually discussed the topic of marriage several times during that summer of 1983, it wasn't until November that Phil actually popped the question. Unsurprisingly I said 'yes' and we married the following March, soon after Phil's twenty-seventh birthday.

Three weeks after our wedding in Richmond, Phil and I moved to the UK as Phil had obtained a job in Oxford. It was there that we settled down into married life. Phil began his job as a research scientist for the University working in the pharmacology department, and I began job hunting. We bought a little terraced house. We joined a lively church and became members of one of the weekly

Bible study groups. Phil also began to make regular visits to the Oxford Haemophilia Centre in order to monitor his haemophilia.

One evening in September 1985, Phil came home from work and told me that tests done at the Haemophilia Centre indicated that his blood contained HIV antibodies. This meant that he was HIV positive. I didn't understand the full implication of this at the time and hung on to the erroneous idea that if he had antibodies his body must be equipped to fight the virus. At this time more and more stories about AIDS were coming into the media but I just didn't want to know. I would turn off the television when a story about AIDS came on, and skip over the topic in magazines. At first it was easy to ignore the fact that Phil was likely to become ill, because our life continued pretty much as normal. We began to talk about starting the family we had planned. At Phil's insistence, we discussed our plans with the staff at the Haemophilia Centre. They gave us information on monitoring cycles so that the risk of infection was minimised as much as possible. Luckily, I quickly became pregnant.

I had routine blood tests but wasn't overly worried about the results. I put this down to my 'head buried in the sand' attitude rather than confidence in God's care. Natasha was born in May 1987 by Caesarean section. The midwives and doctors used barrier nursing to protect themselves and I recovered in the isolation ward while I waited for the results of the tests on Natasha's blood. We were both pronounced antibody free and although I didn't like being relegated to the isolation ward, it had the advantage of being quiet.

Phil was busy at work and at home, besotted with our new daughter. I was so busy learning to look after a new little life that I didn't pay much attention to his persistent cough. Luckily, one of his colleagues at work did and, after a visit to the Haemophilia Centre, he was checked into hospital in the first week in June. The diagnosis was pneumocystis, a form of pneumonia. I wasn't overly concerned until his doctor had a chat with me about the seriousness of his condition. It was then that I finally realised that Phil's cough was connected to the human immunodeficiency virus or HIV that Phil was carrying in his blood. It was a shock and I was finally forced to face the possibility and indeed likelihood of an early death. This likelihood was made more tangible when Phil asked his doctor, 'How long do I have?' 'The average prognosis is three years,' the doctor replied. He also told us a bit about what we could expect. Phil would now be more likely to catch illnesses most people were capable of fighting off. His body would find it more difficult to fight each new illness he contracted, and the time it would take him to recover would become longer each time.

Phil responded well to the medication for his pneumocystis and our life seemed to return to normal although he was taking medication regularly. We concentrated on bringing up our young daughter and Phil continued with his work. It was fortunate in a lot of ways that he was a scientist. His research work endangered no one, and his colleagues, some of them medical doctors, were not likely to panic at the thought of 'catching AIDS'. A second illness that caused Phil to suffer from headaches and double vision occurred in the late spring of 1988.

Again, Phil responded well to treatment. The number of pills he had to take per day was increasing.

In our situation we wanted to concentrate on living as normal a life as possible rather than focus on what the future held. This was why when a job opportunity in Geneva, Switzerland came about in the spring of 1989, I encouraged Phil to go for it. His position in Oxford was temporary and was based on negotiating grants. We were both hoping for something of a more permanent nature. We waited in suspense for the result of the interview and to Phil's amazement he got the job. Before accepting it, he sought advice at the Haemophilia Centre. As always, the director considered the pros and cons and assured us of his support whatever decision we made. His gut feeling, though, was that Phil should go for it.

I felt sure that God had provided this opportunity for a reason and meant us to go to Switzerland. Phil organised for his haemophilia treatment with his new company, deciding not to disclose his HIV status until it became necessary, because he was afraid that this might lead to his being refused employment. We decided to cross those bridges when we came to them.

We travelled to Geneva in November and found a lovely flat to rent. Everything was falling into place, including the beginnings of a friendship with another couple from Oxford, Steve and Simonne, who were moving to Geneva because Steve had found a job working for the same company as Phil. The fact that Steve and Simonne were Christians was another sign to me that God was paving the way for our move to Switzerland.

Everything was proceeding towards the move when Phil became very ill with gastroenteritis soon after our return from Geneva. He went into hospital and I proceeded to organise the move. I still felt sure that God wanted us to go to Geneva although Phil was beginning to have doubts. That Christmas was awful. Phil felt dreadful: he was not only weak but also experiencing a loss of sensation in his legs and feet.

Even so, we left Gatwick for Geneva on 3rd January 1990 after having informed Phil's company that he was not very well. He soon revealed the true nature of his condition at work and I confided in Simonne, needing someone to talk to. After a brief stay in the Hôpital Cantonal, the hospital doctors agreed it would be a good idea for Phil to return to hospital in the UK while matters surrounding his health insurance were sorted out. Two weeks later he returned feeling much better but equipped with crutches and a wheelchair. Thus began our new life in Geneva.

Phil recovered from this illness and responded well to medication but it was not a total recovery. With his strength increasing, he was able to switch from the wheelchair to crutches but the feeling of pins and needles in his feet remained and he did not walk unaided again. He began working, and while he set up his lab, I set about making a home for us in our rented flat in Chêne Bourg. I loved living in Switzerland – the countryside was so pretty and I enjoyed improving my French.

Phil was not enjoying himself as much as I was. He was in constant pain and was always tired. For my part, I tried to find the balance between pushing him to do what I thought he could do in order to lead as normal an existence as possible and letting him get the rest he needed. Phil did not often complain about how awful he was feeling although he was quite vocal about his decrepit body and its limitations.

It was in the summer of 1990 that I finally came to terms with the fact that Phil and I would not be able to have any more children together. Before leaving Oxford, we had visited the consultant in the fertility clinic to ask about methods of fertilisation that would pose the least risk to me. While no method was known to eliminate the risk, other procedures such as sperm washing, might decrease it. I loved being mother to Natasha and wanted more of Phil's children. Because I specifically wanted his children, I had decided not to pursue artificial insemination. Phil had left the decision about whether to have more children up to me, since I would be the one risking infection in the process.

After having talked to the doctors at the hospital, we decided to try for another baby. It was thought that the risk of transmission of the virus was greater after the infected person had developed full blown AIDS. This time I was aware of the consequences, so Phil and I decided that if we did try for another baby, it would only be when the conditions were as favourable as possible: we would both need to be feeling fit and I would need to be ovulating – as far as I could ascertain this by taking my temperature and noting when it rose. Between colds and Phil not feeling 100 per cent, we weren't able to try for our baby very often. Then Phil's gastroenteritis and the move to Geneva occurred, before we had time to follow up our initial talks at the hospital.

I followed the matter up at the hospital in Switzerland, still hoping that some way might be found to have another baby with minimal risk. One day, after taking Natasha to the local playgroup, or *jardin d'enfants* as it was called in French, I was walking home and turning the issues over in my mind when I 'heard' a 'no'. Although my first thought was that this meant, 'No, not now,' in my heart of hearts I knew that this was a 'no' answer to my prayers about having another child. Though not the answer I had wanted, I accepted it as God's will and, although I did not stop *wanting* another child, I was able to stop *fretting* about it.

Phil had become ill yet again after a visit to my family in the States in the summer of 1990. As predicted, the illnesses were coming more frequently and he wasn't bouncing back as he had earlier on. This time TB was suspected. In fact, it turned out to be a micro-organism that caused TB-like symptoms. The constant coughing left Phil feeling weak and tired. He was now not only having regular out-patient visits to the infectious diseases department, but also spending more time as an in patient. This latest bout of illness left him with even more pills to take. 'Sometimes I feel like it's my job to take pills,' he would grumble.

His company, who had been understanding from the ~rt and instrumental in obtaining the health cover we ¹ to stay in Switzerland, installed a computer in our flat so Phil could work from home. That October, we celebrated my thirty-fifth birthday at a lovely restaurant but Phil was too ill to eat much. Over dinner he expressed some of his feelings. In particular he felt sad that he wouldn't see Natasha growing up. There were tears in his eyes as he spoke of this. I was trying to get through one day at a time, while Phil was thinking of the future. One day in early January he gave me the names of some choruses and readings he wanted at his memorial service. 'If it's possible, Boss (the name we called each other), can you spread my ashes on Blencathra?' he asked. Phil loved the Lake District and one of his proudest achievements had been our ascent of Blencathra in the summer of 1985.

That February, we spent a couple of weeks at the Clinique Genevoise in Montana hoping to sort out the diarrhoea that was plaguing Phil and tiring him out. The staff would make an attempt to build him up a bit as well. Phil had never had a big appetite, but now he was finding it difficult to make himself eat at all. As a result, he was steadily losing weight. Although the trip gave us some time away together while Natasha stayed with her grandma in England, the medical aims were unrealised.

It took a colostomy, performed in March, to relieve some of the pressure that had built up in Phil's lower abdomen and stop the diarrhoea. Without having to make constant trips to the toilet, Phil regained a bit of strength and his sense of humour. He seemed closer to being his old self than he had been in months.

However, what we did not realise at first was that the colostomy was only partial. The eruption of Phil's intestine out of the colostomy hole meant another operation in June. It was after that operation that Phil's condition steadily deteriorated. It was almost as if he had given up on getting better; up until that time we had both clung to the hope that a cure would be found. Even so, we planned a two-week holiday with Phil's parents in the south of France at the end of July. By this time it had been four years since Phil's pneumocystis.

The villa Mum and Dad had rented was lovely. I revelled in the dry heat of the Mediterranean, and Natasha was in her element in the swimming pool but Phil was unable to do much except lie in the shade. He couldn't eat solid food and instead drank protein drinks for nourishment. At the end of the two weeks, he was no longer able to read the newspaper. He was also saying strange, inappropriate things, an indication that dementia had set in. He had always worried that the virus would affect his brain and hence his ability to do work. Now it seemed that he was no longer the Phil that I had married.

One late afternoon I took Natasha out for ice cream. I told her that Jesus would probably take Daddy to heaven to make him better. As she seemed to be pleased by that, I told her that this meant Daddy would die.

'I don't want Daddy to die,' she said with tears rolling down her cheeks.

'I don't want him to die either,' I replied. I carefully began to talk with her about who her daddy was – to help her remember him.

The end came in early August, not long after we had returned from our holiday. At a visit to the doctors, we were asked how we felt about prolonging life. Neither of us wanted to use extraordinary measures to keep Phil alive. Having fought long and hard, he was tired and ready to go; and I, by now, was ready to let him go.

On 9th August 1991, I was using the communal washing machine on my allocated day as was customary in Switzerland, while keeping an eye on Phil whom I had moved onto the sofabed in the living room. Friends from church had offered to have Natasha. As the day wore on, Phil's breathing became more and more laboured. His doctor came to the flat and told me that he thought it wouldn't be too long.

I wanted to be with Phil when he died and therefore was determined for him to be at home rather than in hospital. I knew how much he hated hospital and how much he loved home. Besides, with a four-year-old in tow, my time in hospital was limited. By now Phil seemed to have lost consciousness – I noticed his eyes had stopped blinking. I tried to think what kind of music he would like to listen to. Although he had spent many hours in the early part of our courtship trying to convince me of the merits of punk music, I didn't feel this would be entirely appropriate just then. Instead, I inserted a CD of Gustav Holst's *The Planets*, his favourite piece of classical music. Sitting on the sofabed next to him, holding his hand, I told him I was ready to let him go. I whispered that I would teach Natasha about the things he loved. Eventually his breathing grew shallower. Then it ceased – he was gone. To make sure, I dug out Natasha's toy stethoscope to check for a heartbeat and then held a mirror under his nose to see if he was still breathing. He wasn't.

Our church pastor came to help me with the details and as we talked, I found it hard to take my eyes off Phil's body. A doctor came to our flat and provided me with a death certificate. The body was taken away along with some of Phil's best clothes to be used for the funeral. I arranged for Natasha to stay the night with Steve and Simonne and took a walk. The words 'I'm a widow' were going round and round my head as if that would make it more real. At only thirty-four, Phil had died. We had had a short seven years together.

The next day, when Natasha returned, I told her that Daddy had died. She asked me if I was going to die too. We had a cuddle and I replied that I wasn't sick like Daddy had been. We also talked about how Phil was well now, able to run and jump in heaven as he had said he wanted to once he got there.

I knew Phil was in heaven because the Bible promises us

in John 3:16 that those who believe in Jesus will have ever-lasting life. Jesus closed the breach between God and man with his death on the cross and we will live on after we die on this earth just as Jesus did in the resurrection. Because Phil had believed that Jesus was the Son of God and that Jesus had died for his failures and errors, I was able to assure Natasha that her daddy was living with God now. That certainty removed some of the sadness of our loss but I still found it hard to sleep and Natasha threw up several times that night.

There was a lot to arrange in the next few days with Phil's parents arriving from Sevenoaks and my own arriving from America. Phil's sister, Paulette, and her family were flying in from France where they were on holiday, and some friends from Phil's university days who had been planning to see Phil, altered their holiday plans in order to attend his funeral. My church family in Geneva were generous in their offers of hospitality. It was good to have all the arrangements to keep me busy – it kept the awful feeling of numbness at bay.

The service at the crematorium was conducted by our pastor and I had to smile when Natasha asked me when would it be time to go to Sunday school. It was a beautiful summer's day in Geneva and I was borne up by the certainty that Phil was now well and happy.

Once the funeral was over and guests had gone back to their respective homes, life returned to a slower pace. Many things seemed the same – Natasha's routine, going to Migros to get the groceries, housework. But only on the surface. In practical terms, life was suddenly a lot easier for me. Until just before his death, I had nursed Phil myself. This had involved changing his colostomy bags and incontinence pads, encouraging him to eat and drink and carrying him in my arms from our first-floor flat to the car and then, on our return, from the car to our flat. I also needed to carry his wheelchair to and from the car – another trip up and down stairs. The memory of his weak and frail body, weighing only eighty pounds at the time of his death, was still fresh in my mind and I was glad he had been able to leave it behind. The insidious nature of his illness made me recall something Phil had once said, 'No one deserves this disease.'

Although easier in some ways, my life was more difficult in others. I sorely missed having another adult to talk to. Phil and I had found it easy to talk, laugh and solve problems together. I also missed his help with Natasha. Almost up until the end he had helped me by keeping an eye on her and playing with her. I found that battling with a four-year-old was exhausting and I really missed having a back-up.

I thought about what I would do next. I had actually begun thinking about that in Oxford, once it had dawned on me that early widowhood was a distinct possibility for me. I remembered considering the possibilities while wheeling Natasha's push-chair back from the supermarket. Phil had even raised the subject once, asking me whether I would go back to Richmond after he died. But now that he had died, I found myself undecided as to my course of action. In the immediate future, however, I had two projects to occupy me. The first involved organising the memorial service Phil had requested. A date for this was set for 31st August 1991 and a number of Phil's friends had been asked to say something about him. As well as this, there were hymns and readings he had wanted, and others requested by his parents, and a short address by the rector. The service, on a beautiful sunny Oxford summer's day, was uplifting and I even found myself laughing when friends spoke of Phil's dress sense, his kind of humour and his love of films. His strong faith was also spoken of and again I rejoiced that he was in heaven. I thought back to a comment made by my pastor's wife: 'Phil wouldn't want to come back.' While initially shocked by this assertion

('What! Phil not want to come back to me and Natasha?') I soon realised that she was right. Heaven, more wonderful than we can imagine, would be impossible to leave. Moreover, I could believe that Phil would not want to leave the presence of God.

The second project was a book that Hodder and Stoughton had previously asked Phil and myself to write. A writer friend of my in-laws had brought our story to his editor and she had expressed an interest in it. We had submitted some of our thoughts and the project had been given the green light. I now informed the publishers of Phil's death and indicated that I was still keen to go on with the project. They found an accomplished writer to work with me and we were given June 1992 as a completion date.

However, these projects did not address what I was going to do in the more distant future. Switzerland was an expensive place to live and it wasn't easy for foreigners to get jobs. Natasha and I received some money from Phil's company but I was not sure that it would be enough to support myself and Natasha indefinitely. I still owned the house in Oxford and the rent provided me with a small income after the mortgage was deducted. We had opted for a low-start mortgage in 1985 rather than an endowment mortgage. Life insurance had been included for the first three years but then Phil's diagnosis had made a continuation of the policy impossible. I felt that I would probably have to work in order to make our future secure.

But what could I do? My degree in linguistics wouldn't provide me with a career. My working life had been spent in sales, either retail or in the travel industry, but I didn't feel that sales was something I wanted to spend the rest of my life doing. I hit on the idea of taking some time off to retrain. I would be investing in myself. I considered counselling or speech and language therapy. I had initially considered speech therapy as a career while working for my linguistics degree in the late 1970s but had decided against it when my parents, quite within their rights, had said that four years of college tuition was plenty.

Being able to talk with Phil about the future had brought home to me how important communication is. Because we had been able to talk about how we felt, I felt that nothing had gone unsaid and therefore had no regrets on that score. It was one of the few good things that had come from Phil's illness. Good communication was something that had developed gradually between us. For one thing, I had a tendency to sulk when Phil did something I didn't like. I stopped talking to him for two days once, after he had broken one of the dishes we had received as a wedding present! Later, because of the prejudice against people with AIDS, we had been encouraged not to talk to others about it, but within our marriage, communication improved. I found it easier to tell Phil how I was feeling. And, not long before he died, I asked him if he knew what love was. This time he was able to say 'yes'.

After doing some investigation into university courses, I decided to return to England to pursue a course there. I had a number of reasons for not returning to the States: I wanted Natasha to have a sense of where her father had grown up and I was angry with the American government for their policies on people with AIDS – they had requested that any HIV-positive person visiting the USA should declare his status on his passport. I had also grown close to Phil's family over the time I had known them. Natasha and I arrived in Sevenoaks in time for Christmas 1991, our goodbyes to Switzerland said and our furniture in storage.

My book project continued to occupy me and I gained a place on a four-year speech sciences course in London to begin in October. Phil's parents, who had kindly put us up on our arrival, offered us the use of what had been Gran's flat before her death early in 1992. Everything seemed to be falling into place. Having something new to tackle kept me feeling relatively positive. But as time passed, the awful-

ness of Phil's death began to fade slightly from my memory
and I began to miss him more. I missed his hugs and his
touch. I missed his sense of humour. I missed his help with
household jobs. From time to time I felt sorry for myself –
I had to do everything: paying bills, carrying out the
rubbish, taking the car to the garage. I also missed the emotional support that he had given so freely. I felt more keenly
that in Phil, God had provided the perfect husband for me:
someone who had supported me and believed in me; who
had wanted and helped me to be the best that I could be.
Above all, I missed him as a companion. Tears would flow
at odd moments: watching a film we had seen together;
hearing a snatch of music from the early days of our relationship.

In June 1992, I made a trip to the Lake District with Phil's
mum and dad to scatter his ashes on Blencathra as he had
requested. Dad and I climbed the fell, the urn containing
Phil's ashes in a knapsack on my back. Once at the summit,
I removed the urn and lifted the ribbons and seal of the
crematorium, only to find that the lid of the urn was
screwed onto the base. As I had not examined the urn too
closely, I had no way of knowing that I should have
brought a screwdriver! Dad and I collapsed in laughter at
our predicament. Fortunately, we hit on the solution of
using a zip to undo the screws. This accomplished, I gathered handfuls of ashes, which actually looked like small
pieces of white gravel, and flung them across a grassy hill-
side just below the summit. After a short prayer, Dad and
I descended through the mist to the bottom where Mum
was waiting. I felt happy that I had been able to fulfil Phil's
request. I knew that though he had left his mortal body
behind, its remains were in a place he loved.

That autumn, I began the speech sciences course with a
great deal of trepidation. I was thirty-seven years old and
worried that most of my brain cells were long since dead.
Fortunately, as I discovered to my relief, in my year there

was a high number of mature students feeling exactly as I was. I soon adjusted to the routine of commuting to London and studying, although I resented the fact that it limited my time with Natasha, who had started school shortly after our return to England. I joined the church my in-laws attended. Vine Evangelical Church was a friendly fellowship whose members were soon offering practical help. I had known some of the members for years – Phil and I had attended whenever we had visited Mum and Dad. Best of all, I felt that I was seen to be a person in my own right rather than one half of a couple.

The first anniversary of Phil's death passed in August 1992. My book *The Last Mountain – Living with AIDS* was published in January 1993 and with it came a flurry of media attention and speaking engagements. It was liberating to tell people what God had done for me and how he had been with Phil and me throughout my husband's illness.

My course continued. There were times when I ached for Phil and the life we had had before he got ill. Still I knew that our marriage had been stronger because of his illness. Through it we had drawn closer to each other and to God – having to depend on him for his love and care.

I had prayed to God to heal Phil. Soon after Phil's pneumocystis I had asked Rod, the curate at our church in Oxford, what I should pray for. Healing? Skill for the doctors? Relief from pain? Rod assured me that I should pray for healing for Phil and that God wanted him whole. I did this believing that God could cure Phil if it was his will to do so. If Phil were not healed, there had to be a reason, I believed – although I couldn't hope to understand what it was. A Bible study on the Book of Job had really brought home to me the truth that God is in command of the universe. He not only knows what he's doing, but his love for us means that he wants the best for us. In all situations we can trust him. Throughout Phil's illness I was able to hold on to this truth. It helped me not to get angry with God but rather keep on looking forward to the day when I would understand.

I had begun my grieving before Phil's death and thought that this would have given me a head start on getting back to 'normal'. But I soon realised that I still had a great deal more grieving to do. I read some books by other bereaved women which made the point that there is no arbitrary time limit to grieving. This was reassuring because, even now, five-and-a-half years later, I still don't feel normal. I still miss Phil's wonderful sense of humour, his support, his intelligence and the way he accepted people the way they were without trying to change them.

I also miss the romance that was in our marriage. The physical side of our relationship had ceased to exist as Phil's illness had progressed. I had been able to accept this as I cared for his day-to-day needs. But when Phil's youngest sister, Patrina, became engaged in September 1993, all the subsequent wedding plans made me realise just how much I missed being part of a couple. I fought a mostly unsuccessful battle with jealousy and envy and tried to distance myself from the excitement surrounding the wedding in September 1994, hoping this would lessen my misery. I think I was also angry – angry at being left behind. Phil had left me and now Patrina, I felt, was leaving me, even though I realised that she was just getting on with her life. It was a difficult time, that third year of my widowhood. There were no new challenges to tackle and an intense loneliness.

The idea of remarriage had been in my mind even before Phil had died. Indeed, not long before he died, Phil urged me to remarry if I were to find someone I loved. At the time of writing, an opportunity to do that has not yet presented itself. If it did, I would be very pleased, for I would love to marry again. But I am willing to leave the matter in God's hands. I concentrate on the fact that I have a lovely daughter and a rewarding job. Also, I have remained free from infection.

Through the kindness and generosity of people, God has provided me with practical help. He has given me time to adjust to a different kind of life. He has been with me as I've grieved and has given me strength. He has been good to me. I trust him with my future.

Ros's Story

Rosamund Bray (née Volney) is a West Indian who has lived in Britain since 1960. Married twice and widowed twice, she now lives alone in Chislehurst, Kent. She has three married children and three grandchildren, two of whom she cares for three days a week. Before her second marriage, she worked as a legal secretary. She is also involved with her church in Bromley, Kent.

Ros's story was written twelve years after the death of her first husband Gerry and five years after the death of her second, George.

I hid my loneliness. I realised it had an unacceptable face which made other people feel uncomfortable. Soon my 'cover' started to look good, especially when I wore my 'I'm absolutely fine' mask. I attended fitness classes, lost four stone and spent a fortune on trying to give the impression that I was healing nicely. Some friends believed this and told me that I looked a million dollars. Others, I discovered later, knew what was going on and were extremely worried. I also managed to fool myself. But the truth was that I had become very good at hiding the pain.

Ros's Story

I first became aware that something was very wrong indeed when my husband Gerry began to pace the floor of our bedroom at night complaining of severe pain in his side and back. The date was January 1983.

Gerry worked for British Petroleum. We were living in Bickley, Kent, had been married for twenty years and had three children, Maria, Anthony and Charmaine. My husband had previously enjoyed excellent health so his illness came as a massive shock to us.

First, he went to see our GP. After being treated for what was thought to be an ulcer, he was finally referred to a specialist who dealt in stomach disorders. A number of preliminary tests revealed nothing of a serious nature. The doctors were taking no chances however and it wasn't until Gerry went to another hospital where further investigations were carried out that the tumour was found – on the pancreas. It was carefully and gently explained to us that tumours could be malignant or benign.

We were left in no doubt whatsoever that it wasn't a question of *what* to do but *when*. Matters seemed to be escalating at a rate of knots. I well remember this period in my life when our world was just about to be turned on its head with things never likely to be the same again afterwards.

In the week before this, I had experienced a strong

prompting to get a second opinion which would hopefully give us other options. Afterwards I was very grateful that I had backed my intuition, because it resulted in our being seen by a surgeon specialising in diseases of the pancreas and very eminent in his field. We were very fortunate to get an appointment with this man: he was often lecturing abroad or busy with writing or other commitments. Sadly, his diagnosis was identical with the one we had previously been given and we agreed on a date for the operation – 6th April 1983. We were told to go home and spend Easter with our three young children.

I remember having terrible misgivings and being too frightened to voice them to anyone. The unthinkable was at our door, knocking, and my rock of stability was about to be shattered by my learning the truth about his condition. I felt as though my life was breaking up into tiny pieces.

The surgeon made it plain to us both that things were serious and that my husband might have to go into intensive care after the operation. Typically, Gerry took it all in his stride, never once letting on to me or anybody else whether or not he knew just how ill he was. Later I realised that he had honestly believed that whatever the blockage was, it could be removed and he would then be able to resume his life in the normal way.

That was a very long Easter weekend. My heart was heavy and I sensed that we would never again experience family life as we had come to know it. The fear in me was palpable. I could smell it, taste it and even feel it like a tight steel band across my chest. It lived with me all that weekend, giving me no respite. The children, who had a very good relationship with their father and he with them, were completely unaware of all this, and were their cheerful, ebullient selves, fighting and squabbling in typically childlike fashion. There was even laughter to be heard.

From then on we travelled the long, hard, lonely road of

suffering. It was a time of great trial for my husband and myself. He came through the operation but did not go into intensive care. I thought this probably meant that the surgeon had been unable to remove the tumour and had therefore stitched Gerry up again. In fact, as I soon found out, the tumour had been malignant and the surgeon had given him a bypass which would enable him to live, but only for a very limited time.

Gerry, who simply didn't want to know, wasn't told this. But I needed to know the score for myself and ultimately for him, so I cornered one of the surgeons on the team and asked for information. He told me the earth-shattering news that Gerry had between six months and two years to live and that he would be needing me very much over the next months. I suppose my detachment from him and the illness began that day in April. I kept thinking, 'This isn't happening to us.' I even remember that the weather was awful that afternoon – cold and wet, with thunder and sleet – matching my mood.

I remember looking out of the hospital window and beginning to realise that my life as I had known it was over. I felt as though I were on an uphill road strewn with boulders and bordered by deep ravines. I also remember crying out to God, asking him why we had to travel this particular dreadful road. I believe he helped me to see that he had asked his son to tread the path of terrible suffering and that he wasn't asking us to walk our road alone but would accompany us every step of the way. I asked the question why and felt that I received the answer that God loved us. It was extremely hard to assimilate that message, but I believe it was from God because it brought me such peace and comfort. Also, remembering that the awful road to Calvary had ended in resurrection and new life gave me a sense of hope.

We went home and Gerry prepared to convalesce. I wrote to my sister, who lives in America and is a qualified counsellor and psychologist, for advice: Should I tell Gerry that he was going to die quite soon? She wrote back to say that Gerry's body would begin to 'tell' him that all was not well and that then, when he started asking questions, I should hold his hand and tell him the truth. Things happened as she'd said they would and I did as she'd suggested. Telling Gerry the truth was the hardest thing I have ever had to do in my life. And when I had done it, Gerry didn't believe me. He went as white as a sheet but told me that I had got it wrong, and that the surgeon, with whom he had an appointment the following day, would put me right. I looked at him and loved him – that was all I could do. The children knew that their father was very ill but, like him, they lived in denial and carried on as normal. I suppose I ought to have been grateful for that, but I wasn't. I felt like screaming at them, 'Don't you realise that you are going to lose your daddy?' But of course I didn't. I kept my own counsel.

Next day the surgeon, far from putting me right as Gerry had hoped, confirmed our worst fears. As we left Harley Street, I remember thinking that we must have looked as though we had had too much to drink. I don't know how we got ourselves home. I was pretty sure that now that Gerry had had to accept the prognosis, things would get more difficult. This proved to be the case. My husband became impossible to live with. This once placid person who had taken everything in his stride, became unkind, demanding and angry. The illness, of course, took its toll. During the last year of his life, Gerry suffered considerable losses of blood, starving his brain of oxygen, and catapulting him into comas. He was in and out of hospital practically every month having transfusions. Many times he almost died.

One night preparations were made for his imminent death which was expected before morning. I sat up all night at his bedside and helped when he was given the last rites. But at 5 am I began to plead with God to allow Gerry to remain with us for a while longer so that he could help our son as he faced exams and, later, job applications. Gerry had been in a coma for most of the night but after praying this prayer I spoke softly but firmly to him, telling him that there was work for him to do and insisting that he should come back and do it. Eventually he opened his eyes, looked straight at me and asked, 'What work are you talking about?' I felt overwhelmed: God had heard my entreaties.

My husband then asked for a drink. When the surgeon came onto the ward the next morning, he was completely mystified by what had happened; so were the nursing staff. I believe that it was a miracle. By mid-morning Gerry was sitting up in bed, drinking orange juice through a straw, reading *The Times* and welcoming astonished close relatives who had heard that he was dying and had come to see him for the last time. He actually died six months later but by then we were as ready as it is possible to be in such circumstances. I was deeply grateful to God for the extension of time that we had. In the dark days prior to Gerry's death, my faith carried me through, as God helped me directly and through his people.

I had the support of many wonderful friends who somehow always managed to appear at the house at just the right moment; when I was having to go up to the hospital as an emergency leaving the children on their own, for example. They also cooked, cleaned, prayed for us and generally loved us throughout Gerry's illness. One particular friend gave me her time and love consistently over the whole of those two years, demonstrating God's loving care in a wonderful way. So there were special aspects of those painful, difficult days.

While Gerry was convalescing and before he learnt of his impending death, he kept disappearing on Sunday mornings. I assumed that he went off to his golf club but, to my amazement, discovered instead that he had been checking out the local churches. In the end he informed me that he thought that the Catholic church was the one for him and asked me to arrange for him to have the relevant instruction. You could have knocked me over with a feather! Up to that time, Gerry had not been 'religious', whereas I was by this time a practising Christian, worshipping at St Joseph's Catholic Church, Bromley. I had not been so when we had first married in 1963, but six months before the cancer had struck, I had been converted. I believe that at that time God also gave me a wonderful gift of faith – undeserved but very much needed for what was to come.

Anyway, Gerry became a Roman Catholic and was baptised in June 1984. In May the following year, he died, having lived two years and one month after the original diagnosis. It happened very early one sunny May morning. After a long, hard struggle, and while he was saying the Lord's Prayer, he slipped into his final coma and went to meet his creator. The doctor attending him at the time said, 'He is on the home run now.' I never forgot those words, which I have treasured ever since.

Coping with the death of a loved one is one thing; coping with the grief afterwards is another. My friends did their best to help me 'get my act together', through reassurance, gentle persuasion and conveying 'spiritual truths'. Some told me that I had the same resources as they had and that, with their help and love, I ought to be able to function normally. Others put pressure on me to admit my need, but sometimes asking for help made me feel silly, inadequate or even guilty. In the end, I tried to keep everything inside.

I hid my loneliness. I realised it had an unacceptable face which made other people feel uncomfortable. Soon my 'cover' started to look good, especially when I wore my 'I'm absolutely fine' mask. I attended fitness classes, lost four stone and spent a fortune on trying to give the impression that I was healing nicely. Some friends believed this and told me that I looked a million dollars. Others, I discovered later, knew what was going on and were extremely worried. I almost managed to fool myself. But the truth was that I had become very good at hiding the pain.

I realised that some people wanted me to be strong for their sakes. The more I hid my true feelings, the more relieved and secure they felt and the better they coped. I observed them incredulously, wondering why I still felt so empty and hopeless. Inside my head at times, certain words and ideas seemed to scream at me along the lines of: 'Hide at all costs! My friends must be protected from me. I must be protected from me. I am a nuisance.'

At the same time, some of my relatives were pressuring me to deny the extent to which my life had changed. They wanted me to put up a good front, present a quiet exterior, be serene, controlled and smiling. They reminded me that I had children to think about, whose needs must come before my own. They told me not to worry about the future and seemed to have no understanding that for me the future looked endless and frightening and full of uncertainty. I felt I had lost control of my life; I was afraid, not knowing what would happen. Looking ahead was like looking into an abyss.

Some people insisted that I should visit Gerry's grave every week. I kept protesting about this, pointing out that Gerry wasn't there, but to no avail. Finally my elder daughter became so exasperated that she exclaimed one day, 'Mum cannot jump into the grave with Dad!' Apart from not knowing what I was supposed to do at the grave, I also felt that I was being kept tied to someone who no longer existed physically, instead of being able to start facing the reality of grief and of my loss and aloneness.

As far as my faith was concerned, I felt I ought not to indulge in expressing my anger and grief, because God, so

I had been taught, was good. But at the time, God became more and more remote because I was finding it increasingly difficult to accept that his plan for my life included separating a husband and father from his family. I felt that he had taken a part of me that I treasured and desperately needed. But because I believed that God was God and his actions were not to be questioned, I repressed my pain, anger and sense of injustice.

Then, one day, someone asked me, 'Ros, have you had a nitty gritty conversation with Jesus about this?' My first reactions were mixed. However, because I trusted this person, I went to church one day when nobody else was around and poured out my heart to God for about an hour. Anger, resentment and all sorts of similar emotions came tumbling out. Of course God was silent. I don't know what I had been expecting. But what I got, after all the talking and crying, was deep peace – an awareness that God understood it all and would take care of everything; that he would be true to his word.

Daily life had to continue and it soon dawned on me that as far as society was concerned, I had lost my status. At the same time I had a great many new and daunting tasks to do. There were many complicated and, to me, terrifying forms to be filled in, and I kept having to designate myself as a widow. When papers were returned, there were often errors or spelling mistakes in them, and Gerry's name continued to appear on letters and forms. Funeral arrangements and decisions about a plot of land for burial had to be dealt with efficiently and speedily, so I was fortunate in having a friend to help me with those.

I found the finances very difficult and frightening, but I didn't like to admit my feelings of inadequacy, so put on a good front. The reality was that things got so bad that I couldn't even bring myself to open bank statements when they arrived. And I was spending money like water, buying lots of clothes and doing a good deal of travelling.

It helped to dull the inner pain for a time – but then this would flare up as fiercely as ever. I finally had no option but to come to grips with the finances: it was a case of sink or swim. My son proved invaluable, spending hours helping me with these. One of the first things he encouraged me to do was to write down all my credits and debits. Had I done this at the beginning, I would have saved myself hours of agony and worry. But one lives and learns and I learnt many valuable and important lessons.

If I were to sum up this period in my life, I would say that although my emotions were up and down like a yo-yo and I felt frightened most of the time, my true friends were towers of strength for me and remained faithful to me. I owe it to them that I survived and recovered so very well.

I met my second husband George at a Bible study group at our church. He was a retired stockbroker and a widower. I was by then forty-seven years old, feeling much better and wanting to marry again. In fact, I had asked God to find me a husband! He was to have two specific and principal qualities: he must love God first and foremost, but also love me 'to bits'!

God answered my prayer wonderfully but at first I thought he had got his wires crossed. George was twenty-two years older than I was and no Cary Grant! When he began making tentative advances, I wasn't too keen at first, not recognising him as the person chosen for me because he didn't fit my image of who I wanted. But, as I was to discover, God's plans are always better than ours and exceed anything we could dream up on our own.

To my great and utter happiness, I very soon discovered that George and I shared not only spiritual closeness but also a love of music. More than that, we both played the piano – he like a master. It was the icing on the cake when we discovered that, as well as the classics, we both liked the music of the 1930s and 40s with the big bands and extremely talented songwriters such as Gershwin, Cole

Porter, Fats Waller, Count Basie, Duke Ellington, Rodgers and Hammerstein to name but a few! We had so much in common, and to say that George loved me would be a very big understatement. We married in December 1988.

To say that we were very happy would also be an understatement. George even wrote songs for me. We discussed at great length every subject we were ever interested in. We seemed to know that we didn't have a great deal of time and so we lived each day to the full. Our music was an enormous source of joy to us. We had a piano each and would play together (not duets, but the same pieces) so the combined sound was very melodic – at least the people who complimented us on our prowess seemed to think so! George played in his style and I in mine. He played from memory and I by ear; he read music and I didn't. So, I believe, we complemented each other on the piano and made beautiful music together in our lives as well.

After our year of courtship, we had three ecstatic years together. Our marriage brought us both completely unexpected happiness and deep joy on a level that neither of us had experienced before. George was a man much loved by all who knew him.

When I first met George, I was feeling like a worn, battered old painting, dull and lacking lustre. Over the next four years George lovingly and painstakingly restored me, showing me God's extravagant love in hundreds of ways. On Valentine's Day, masses of flowers would be delivered to the door – something I had never experienced before. As well as enjoying the flowers and all the other gifts, I learnt that God too is a generous giver and longs to lavish good things on his beloved.

George's death came unexpectedly in 1992. The specialist who had told me about Gerry's cancer now said that George had cancer in his lungs and in his liver. It was another devastating blow for me – one which I hadn't expected so soon after Gerry's death only six years earlier.

We had three weeks to prepare for George's death. He told me that he didn't feel he could ask God for any more time, because he saw it as God's generosity that he had fallen in love at the age of seventy-one. He knew something of his creator and reflected many aspects of him and his love. I will be forever grateful to him for that, and because he helped to heal me of hurts from my first marriage and assisted me with my children who grew to love him dearly. When he lay dying in the hospital, my friends mounted a round-the-clock vigil by his bedside so that he would never be alone. This meant that I could snatch a couple of hours of sleep or rest at nights. I shall never forget their love and commitment to us in this and other ways. Our parish priest came to administer the last rites and to pray. Two other priests, who were friends, also came and prayed with us. Afterwards, one of them said he had been at many death-beds but had never seen a death like George's. My husband was truly a holy man.

At George's funeral, there wasn't even standing room in the church. During the service I was given permission to play 'One o'clock Jump' by Count Basie over the church's loudspeaker system. The whole service was a fitting end for a wonderful man.

Five years have now elapsed, and life has settled down again. The children are a wonderful legacy from my first husband. My grandchildren are blessings. The memories have become kinder and I have learnt to like myself and enjoy who I am. My inner life with God sustains me on a daily basis and my friends are a great source of joy and fun to me.

For some years now, I have been helped and inspired by a spiritual director. He too has shown me God's love by his care of me in my widowhood. All in all, I enjoy life and am grateful for all that has happened because I wouldn't be the person I am today if I had not experienced what I have. And I want to say that it is possible to come out of the tunnel of grief and, yes, there is a bright light at the end. I give thanks to the one who made it all possible. 'By his stripes [I am] healed' (Isaiah 53:5). 'He has kept [my] feet from slipping' (Psalm 66:8).

Jennie's Story

Jennie Juckes farmed in Mid Wales in partnership with her husband for over thirty years. Within the space of two years, she sustained the loss of her husband and of most of their farm. She now lives in the farmhouse which she kept along with twenty acres of the land. She has three adult children, and has been accepted as a counsellor with the churches' counselling services in Wales.

Jennie's story was written two and a half years after the death of her husband Peter.

How lightly, thoughtlessly, as it now seems to me, we say things like 'at a stroke' or 'I nearly had a stroke'! For Peter, having a stroke meant that he went from reasonable if limited mobility, to comparative immobility; from freedom to captivity; from being able to fend for himself to not being able to do anything for himself; from actively caring for others to being on the receiving end of constant care from them. I could only surmise his bewilderment, confusion and subsequent frustration. Despite that, his patience and dignity were impressive. He grew in stature. The ordinary structures of daily life disappeared, but the four of us all pulled together, our arms around each other.

Jennie's Story

In 1993, my husband Peter took the decision to have a first hip replacement. In view of his rather poor medical history, it was a courageous one. My hope was that he would be scheduled early on the surgeon's list, but he was put at 12.30 pm – last.

'It makes no difference,' the ward sister responded to my protests. The next day, about an hour before the operation was due, I was walking through the town, when a cry of anguish for Peter wrenched my heart. I quickly returned to his cousin's house where I was staying, entering it just in time to hear the phone ringing.

'That's Peter!' I thought. Instead the sister's voice told me, 'Your husband has had a slight stroke. He is still conscious. We can't do the hip replacement now.'

After the shock came the realisation that I had in some way picked up on Peter's distress – experiencing that mysterious unity between husband and wife, in which communication takes place at very deep, incomprehensible levels.

How lightly, thoughtlessly, as it now seems to me, we say things like 'at a stroke' or 'I nearly had a stroke'! For Peter, having a stroke meant that he went from reasonable if limited mobility, to comparative immobility; from freedom to captivity; from being able to fend for himself to not being able to do anything for himself; from actively caring for others to being on the receiving end of constant care from them. I could only surmise his bewilderment, confusion and subsequent frustration. Despite that, his patience and dignity were impressive. He grew in stature. The ordinary structures of daily life disappeared, but the four of us all pulled together, our arms around each other.

Several months later, Peter came home, able to speak well but now in a wheelchair – much disabled by a combination of the stroke and arthritis. The following year a skilled surgeon did the postponed hip replacement on his paralysed side. Peter amazed the orthopaedic staff by his determination to regain as much movement as he possibly could. Overjoyed that, thanks to the hip replacement, he would at least have less pain to bear, we glimpsed wider horizons for him.

Ten weeks later an accident landed him back in casualty with what we feared was a hip dislocation. His condition deteriorated, necessitating an emergency abdominal operation. Gravely ill, he was transferred straight away to the Intensive Therapy Unit. Two weeks later, on 15th September 1994, he died at the age of fifty-seven.

In spite of considerate and thoughtful reassurance from dedicated hospital staff, right from the outset of his stay in ITU, I sensed that Peter had had enough. He had never advocated hanging on to life at all costs. All I asked for was God's mercy for him, whatever that might mean, vowing that I would not shirk staying with him, no matter what the outcome. A relative of Peter's who was also a priest had come to be with us and I remember him saying quietly to me, 'Sometimes the dying are holding on for the family's sake – just waiting for their permission to let go. It is a gift then if we can say, "I care for you so much more than I care for myself that I will let you go, if you so wish."'

The day after I heard these words, Peter died. With children and close friends, I walked out of the hospital into the evening light. My thoughts and emotions had been thrown into wild disorder. Previously, leaving the hospital had meant leaving Peter behind. On this occasion, I could not speak because I felt so clearly that Peter was coming with us, freed from the paraphernalia of high-tech equipment.

In the coming days, weeks and months, Peter filled all my waking moments and my fragmented, dream-torn sleep. There was no room for other considerations – apart from his children; and his brothers – dear representatives of him and yet not him. 'Peter! Peter!' was my every thought. Emotions raged and ranged in great confusion – unidentifiable.

In the initial weeks, I was lost in a wilderness where there were no signposts. Emptiness extended in every direction across a devastated landscape into a seemingly endless, unwished-for future. How could I cope with an event I had always so dreaded? The inconceivable had happened. What could I hold on to? Even through the sharp lacerations of pain, I never lost the certainty that God would pull me through. I held tightly to that belief. I knew it was a question of either swimming or drowning in grief – the kind of grief which scatters coherent thinking and functioning.

But in the darkness and confusion, one signpost did become visible to me. In the forefront of my mind was the conviction that I had to meet my pain head on – entering its granite grip, trying to break it down into separate fragments. For Peter's sake, as a way of honouring him, I would tackle this task, even welcome it. And perhaps as I did so, I would begin to recover and gain new perspective. At first, I did not allow for the possibility that I might ever find meaning or pleasure again: my remaining years would simply have to be endured – nothing more. How that time was to be occupied was another matter.

Far too soon, as I now realise, I grasped at the idea of giving as a way of repaying others for their immeasurable support. My prayer was, 'Lord, my pain is bottomless: let me stand with others in their times of trial.' Someone cautioned me to wait. Another suggested, 'Look after yourself first.' Such common sense, so needed in what I felt to be a senseless world, steadied my feelings of wild rotation and disorder.

'Slow down and listen to yourself and to others,' I counselled myself. 'Pay attention to your inner voice.' And so the rush to give, the first urgent desire, faded into the background, became unattractive even for the time being. My 'offering' needed to be reshaped and purified by God; needed the furnace of grief before it could be softened, hammered, moulded.

After the funeral, home on the farm, I made two choices about how to use some of my unwanted time. I would go for walks and I would begin writing 'letters' – putting down my thoughts and feelings. Perhaps these would help me to wrest some kind of meaning out of despair.

I realised that I could not step into the future without attending to and absorbing the past. One way in which I tried to do this was by 'searching' for Peter, touching places and things where he had been, sighing, repeating his name. In these ways I mourned his passing.

Something else from our shared past was our exploration of silence and solitude. Together and separately, we had gone on retreats, discovering that silence was a friend that brought delight and refreshment of spirit as we drew near to God. But after Peter's death things were different. The silence which had once brought blessings now rang with emptiness and absence. I felt abandoned in it. The pain I felt was gritty, bruising, sweaty, a crucifixion of my inner being, which left me feeling like half a person, raw at the edges. But I persisted, trusting that healing would come in time. I walked for miles in all kinds of weather, desperately searching for answers even as I scanned the ether and the hedgerows for traces of Peter.

I learnt that considerable time is needed before the heart

156 PATHWAY THROUGH GRIEF

can cope with reality. Facts are taken in, but often not assimilated. On the contrary, they may be strongly denied. I experienced something of this unreality and denial. Another, later, response was outrage and rebellion against the abrupt end to the God-promoted relationship of our marriage; the sudden cut-off which allowed no further communication. We had suffered the severest of trials but there was to be no debriefing or follow-up. Peter had gone and there were no clues, no postcard even, to tell of his arrival anywhere else.

My 'letters' to Peter and to God dealt in some measure with unfinished business between the two of us, affirming on paper my love and my despair, discharging emotion in passionate language to a vanished husband and invisible God. Even though silence was not yet proving the friend it had been, I felt I should stay with it, sure that I would eventually learn new truths from it. After all, countless seekers have courted it and written of its treasure. The Welsh poet and priest, R. S. Thomas, puts over the idea of 'trying to analyse the silence' and asks, 'Does God hide in the silence?' So I continued to embrace it that first year. Not that I never went out: invitations were offered and I accepted them. But the television and radio remained unused.

At times my quest was rewarded. Sometimes the silence was deep, full of God's presence. Then tranquillity surrounded me. Outside the trees shimmered with golden light, their soundless beauty seeming to mirror the peace which was offered me. But there were other times when inconsolability engulfed me. Then I could not remain alone, but rushed out to friends and spiritual helpmates, begging that they would generously give me of their time. Because I had read in the New Testament, and experienced for myself, that Christians do share each other's burdens, I had little hesitation in seeking out fellowship.

There were times when I felt abandoned and desolate –

able to identify in that sense with Jesus crying out from the cross, 'My God, my God, why have you forsaken me?' Spiritual counsel was then essential for my survival so I drew heavily on the resources of others. My parish priest and other spiritual helpmates did not fail me. Like other bereaved people, I needed and sought attentive listeners: those who understood that the endless repetition of traumatic details is not a waste of time but therapeutic – a significant part of the recovery process.

Something particularly distressing which I had to deal with was the way Peter had died. Unbidden graphic action replays crowded my mind from his time in ITU and the events leading up to this. I continued to roam the fields and hills and to write in order to alleviate some of the images and the pain. Words poured out as I relived Peter's last days and moments.

Gradually, almost imperceptibly, the emotional rollercoaster of my feelings began to stabilise. I believe this was because at a deep level within me, God was calming things down. It then became possible for feelings to surface and be identified and expressed.

One of my emotions was anger: not against death which must come to all of us but, irrationally perhaps, at the divine institution of marriage which, if successful, must end in heartbreak. I felt anger too at my inability to pierce the veil – to comprehend God in his divine light. He was, as one hymn puts it, 'inaccessible, hid from our eyes'.

My longing for Peter, which was not assuaged and which I could never envisage being so, also led to anger in one form or another at times. Quite unreasonable indignation filled me when the initial 'P' no longer appeared on the envelopes bearing our incoming mail, when I heard myself designated as a widow, or when people said, 'Peter is dead,' rather than, 'Peter has died.' The former, I felt, had a terrible finality about it, while the latter implied more of a transition, a possible continuity.

Remorse pierced with guilt were other early feelings along the lines of: 'If only during our married life I had understood you better!' Illness had brought compassionate understanding into our relationship. But mourning his death created in me a deeper capacity for empathy which I would dearly like to have had beforehand. True and false feelings of failure cut me to pieces.

A month after Peter's death, I took a break at a retreat centre in the majestic Brecon Beacons. The friendly, compassionate nuns there knew us both well. I spoke about my persistent feelings of remorse. They suggested an imaginative exercise. I was to invite Jesus Christ and Peter into my room and then, in their words, 'See what you say – see what they say.' When I did this, I experienced a strong realisation, almost like a message from him, that Peter now fully understood our life together and me – and I remembered that in eternity we would 'know as we are known'. Where such full understanding exists, there can be no blame. This insight brought me joy; I cried and laughed from sheer relief. My wound, previously infected with remorse, could now begin to heal cleanly. This was the first real turning point in my path through grief.

Laughter and weeping continued to mingle as the children shared memories with me. There was a tension involved here: part of me wondered how I could be merry when my whole being wanted to grieve for and pay tribute to Peter. Perhaps it's harder to mourn properly in the West where the expression of sorrow is minimised, whereas weeping and wailing at funerals are normal in some other parts of the world. The unnatural stifling of grief could make for incomplete mourning, adding to feelings of agitation and frustration. I found ways of releasing my grief and of paying tribute to Peter – by walking and writing, thinking and talking, staying at home or going out.

I still went on the occasional retreat. The experience of being there felt very different now but I went in trust that

God could draw very close as I came to him in deep suffering and that such encounters could lead to 'amendment of life and the grace and comfort of the Holy Spirit'. They were also one of the contexts in which I could release feelings appropriately. Kind friends sometimes try to prevent bereaved people from letting their feelings out in the mistaken belief that getting in a state is bad for them; or, failing that, they attempt to put the lid on things as quickly as possible by offering inappropriate or at least untimely comfort or diversions. These don't assist us in coming to terms with or accepting our loss. On the contrary, I found it beneficial, at times, to have a good yell. I would do this in the car, for the sake of my long-suffering dogs and cats. This kind of passionate release helped me.

To say that I wrote and walked may make these activities sound facile, but for me they involved hard, painful effort; certainly they were not a waste of time or an exercise in fruitless morbidity. Gradually the intervals between the entries in my 'correspondence' grew longer. Rereading them, I realise that the process came to a natural halt a month after the second commemoration of Peter's death on the day that would have been our thirty-seventh wedding anniversary. Perhaps I can now say that my decision to live alone in order to face my sorrow with God's grace seems to be working. From what I have written, I can discern patterns in which abysmal darkness was shot through with shafts of light and moods swung repeatedly between belief and disbelief, hope and doubt. The constant repetition of those themes with variations was necessary to my recovery; to regaining my emotional health, learning to live with gradually healing scars.

I ponder over a mystifying verse in Hebrews: 'In bringing many sons to glory – it was fitting that God, for whom and through whom everything exists, should make the author of their salvation perfect through suffering' (Hebrews 2:10). If this applied to Jesus, should it not in some measure apply to us? Not that our sufferings can be redemptive in anything like the sense in which Jesus' were, but that they can bring about unique insights and a change of heart.

Towards the end of the second year, it seemed as though the first act of our tragedy ended. The role I had undertaken, as Peter's representative, to be strong for others and to comfort them, faded. The other players departed to be absorbed back into their usual routines but I was left centre stage with no part to resume. It was then that loneliness enveloped and threatened to destroy me. I resolved to face this, too, head on. Focusing on it with God's help, I could perhaps turn it to good account. Maybe this thick cloud of misery could be turned inside out to reveal the proverbial silver lining. Within the loneliness, I found fear: fear of not coping, of responsibilities, of ill health, of going over the edge. I also found self-pity compounded by a feeling of worthlessness. I longed to be affirmed, to feel special again. I longed for any company, especially in the evenings, missing particularly the masculine element in my life – if I can put it that way. I longed for affirmation of the sort that, with Peter gone, was no longer possible. I saw myself as hugely inadequate and weak and, for those reasons, felt afraid of the future.

As, inevitably, the number of visitors to my house declined, so my difficulty in handling loneliness increased. It was my choice to remain in the house by myself and to face what I felt rather than spending a lot of time away, which was only a way of escape that solved nothing, since I always had to return. In all this, my dogs and cats were a great help; they were always unreservedly overjoyed to see me, whatever my mood. Something else which helped was a book which encouraged me to make living alone an inward journey to fellowship. The writer spoke of loneliness as a great opportunity and as fertile ground for spiritual growth and abundance. My spirit lifted and was exhilarated by all this. God could be invited to fill the void inside me, replacing the negative things. I had learnt from past experience that this dear God of ours, willed to give us greater freedom by accompanying us through our worst fears. For Peter to die was my worst fear realised. But I could respond by going into my inner room, closing the door and praying to my Father who was unseen. With this new approach and frame of mind, I accepted the challenge of using loneliness as an opportunity to go deeper into my relationship with God and my own self-understanding.

Despite my attempt to deal with my inner thoughts, I was not unaware of my surroundings. I have always observed and been affected by the cycle of the seasons. Winter in the magnificent foothills of Snowdonia necessitates battening down the hatches in the worst storms. The long dark, from November onwards, seemed so often to reflect my unhappy thoughts. Spring, in joyful re-creation, aroused a very different response in me – one of delight. Yet in the first couple of springs following Peter's death, the joy was clouded with sadness. We had retained twenty acres after selling most of the farm in May 1994. As I walked about, images of Peter leapt out of every corner of our land; of a strong, able young man, thrilled to bits with the purchase of his own farm in a beautiful, borderland county.

I am learning that God can transform the sadness of memories into forward-looking thankfulness. I believe the seasons show us the person behind the scenery: the creator. Winter, for all the apparent deadness of vegetation, contains the essence and beginnings of new life. Exquisite spring is brimful of that life. Chiffchaffs and curlews enchant the ear. The long-awaited swallow arrives. The sun slants brightly through new green growths and across swathes of primroses, violets and bluebells. Then comes summer, bringing in fragrance and glorious profusion, followed by autumn with its amazing generosity and abundance, yet carrying undertones of decay and mortality. One season contains the traces of another as darkness yields to light and fruitfulness.

I needed much help before my spiritual and emotional darkness could yield to light and fruitfulness. One thing I did was to continue to go to church in the nearby village, as if grasping a lifeline. There I was welcomed back into the loved familiar; it was like receiving salve for my hurt. The congregation, in look and speech, were Christ's ambassadors to me. The actual words were not crucial, but it was their empathic willingness to come alongside me in my loss of Peter which signified so much. The loved familiarity of the often maligned Anglican liturgy held me, cradled me, and soothed me like a well-known lullaby. The liturgy made me a participant in prayer when I could not formulate my own prayers or worship. Texts from Scripture or words from the liturgy would unexpectedly be highlighted, making real to me again the promises of God.

'. . . through Jesus Christ our Lord, who by his death has destroyed death': hearing this from the *Book of Common Prayer*, I was struck afresh with the truth that death is not the finality it seems. 'Therefore with angels and archangels and with all the company of heaven, we laud and magnify thy glorious name, evermore praising thee and saying . . .': as I heard the ringing tones of the celebrant saying these words, my spirit lifted as I was reminded of, and helped to reaffirm my belief in, resurrection and life after death. My struggle with loneliness, as well as compelling me to seek out and benefit from Christian fellowship, began to offer opportunity instead of despair. My hope is that God will keep me going down this road.

After Peter died, I would sit for hours in great abstraction of mind. I think this was ultimately helpful, if not obviously so at first, for I was involved in sorting and sifting my emotions. My inner 'room' was full up with Peter: I was completely preoccupied with him and with trying to find answers to questions concerning where and how he was. As I became less caught up with these matters and faced the realities of my situation, my inner room echoed with emptiness. But I had been given a new perception on that emptiness and while continuing to be open to God's work within it, I also began to turn outwards and into the community. I began to see people in a new way. They were not just there to meet my neediness or to satisfy my urge to give. They were unique individuals to be known, valued and enjoyed in their own right. My desire to give – in terms of pastoral work and neighbourliness – returned, but now I felt that what I wanted to offer had changed and would continue to change as I kept learning and growing.

I have received so much that it is impossible to list or recall all of it. But I was greatly helped and comforted by relatives and friends who telephoned consistently – especially in the evenings; friends who sat beside me in church; friends who included me in their families; lunch invitations – in fact, any invitations; photographs of Peter arriving in the post; people who talked about Peter; flowers on anniversaries or at any other time; people who came to listen time and again; the friend who planted a tiny oak to replace the huge oak which in time would die and which Peter had loved so much; all my contacts with my sons and my daughter and with my husband's brothers.

The writer of Ecclesiastes tries to find sense in a troubled, perplexing world. Now at a distance of two and a half years on I find it easier to understand his interpretation of meaningless. He speaks of 'a time to be born and a time to die', and 'a time to mourn and a time to laugh'. Almost against my will, I find the latter coming true. My own personal addition to the list might be: 'a time to receive and a time to give'. One thing is certain, that Peter would want us to 'get over' his death in the sense of not pining for ever but rather moving forward in hope. I do not like or approve of what happened to him, but I begin to accept it. He cannot speak for himself, yet it is almost as though I can 'hear' him. C. S. Lewis in *A Grief Observed* writes of experiencing the presence of his wife Joy after her death as a meeting of minds. There are rare moments in which I fleetingly experience something akin to this with Peter.

I remember the day in May 1993 when Peter drove us to the hospital. Trying to reassure one another, we chanted together some words of the mystic Julian of Norwich: 'All things shall be well' and 'You shall see for yourself that all manner of things shall be well.' Subsequent terrible events seemed to be a complete contradiction of that, but only perhaps because I was trying to do the impossible: comprehend divine mysteries with my finite mind and perspectives. One such mystery I am content to believe in – God's complete and boundless love for us.

John's Story

John and Sheila Miller returned to Northern Ireland in June 1994 after twenty-four years with OMF International. During the 1970s they taught missionaries' children at Chefoo School, Malaysia. In January 1982 they moved to Singapore where John worked as a director for OMF International. Sheila spent much of her time writing books and leading Bible studies for Jewish women.

John is now a minister-at-large with OMF International. He has a baby granddaughter, born to his son Jonathan, who is the BBC World Service correspondent for Indo-China.

John's story was written ten months after the death of his wife Sheila.

The graveside service in the historic cemetery was short. The sense of the enemy-ness of death in depriving us of our loved one was profound as the orchids and daffodils were placed on the grave. Jonathan and I stood, arms on each other's shoulders. 'Pray now, Dad,' he urged as we gazed on those flowers and through tears thanked our loving heavenly Father for giving us such a radiant woman as wife and mother.

John's Story

Sheila had written nine books. Her final work was to rewrite an earlier poem for use in the worship she led at OMF's Concern for China Conference in November 1995.

Commitment

I once was a bride,
I'll not forget that day!
Sunshine and a singing heart
Had come my way.

I recall roses.
My snowy gown's soft fall,
The red church but – most of all
My groom so tall.

That was long ago.
Just memories are left
Of laughter, love and tears in
Life's warp and weft.

Yet! Another day
Will dawn from heaven fair.
A slain Lamb will claim His bride,
And I'll be there!

Right? We'll all be there!
In wedding gowns be met.
Our Groom, the precious Son of God,
Will not forget . . .

At the end of her poem Sheila had written, 'N. B. *Still to be worked on.*' However, the master craftsman's work on her was just about complete, but not before one final severe illness. It started very suddenly on 23rd November 1995. Initially it did not appear to be serious. Our GP said Sheila had flu. She was confined to bed in our home in Saintfield, County Down.

Sheila's flu quickly developed into pneumonia. When both lungs became affected, our doctor decided she should go into a small hospital 'for a few days'. There her condition rapidly deteriorated, necessitating a move to Belfast City Hospital. That same afternoon, Tuesday 5th December, Sheila was transferred to the Intensive Care Unit (ICU). The next day our son Jonathan arrived from Bangkok where he worked as the BBC's World Service correspondent. By Friday 8th December, doctors thought Sheila had 'turned the corner'. The next day she was able to sit on a chair for an hour and her doctor said he aimed to have her home for Christmas. Our spirits were high. Sheila asked me to send cards to four of her friends who had December birthdays. Now I'm so glad I did, for that was one of the last things Sheila asked me to do for her – that and a phone call to her friend Jean Watson, whose husband had died suddenly two months earlier. 'Ask Jean how she's doing. Don't talk about me,' she said. 'I want to know how Jean is coping.'

On Sunday 10th December, Sheila was drowsy and kept falling asleep, propped in a sitting position in bed. Little did I know that I'd never hear her voice again. An hour after leaving her, I had a phone call to tell me that Sheila had been put on life support. That signalled the beginning of a horrendous experience. Consultants told Jonathan and me next day that Sheila had become very seriously ill. The prognosis was very poor. Breathing was Sheila's major difficulty. To me, Sheila's pale motionless face indicated neither improvement nor decline. Gradually Jonathan and I became used to reading the battery of machines that measured her physical condition. I was fast becoming a dial-and-screen-gazer, desperately missing the personal interaction with Sheila.

On Monday 18th December, an attempt was made to take Sheila off the drugs. She began to wake up but was in great distress. She was trying to cough but was unable to because of the ventilator tube in her throat. Her face was red and swollen. Her eyes were glazed, yellowed and partially open. They moved fractionally as I comforted her. It was terrible to watch. I told her, 'This must be awful, darling, but it is actually a sign you are improving that the doctors are taking you off the drugs.' I held her hand and tried to encourage her – but she soon had to be put back on the drugs. She never again came off them.

That night a crisis developed when her heart rate plummeted. Warning bells rang. Even though unconscious, Sheila's face registered alarm. I was told to leave as doctors and nurses rushed to her. Sheila clawed her way out of danger. I waited outside the entrance door to Intensive Care. I came to dread that long winding corridor which led to ICU. As I entered it now and every morning, I was gripped by fears of what I would find when I arrived at Sheila's bedside again.

At 2.30 am on Saturday 23rd December, the night nurse in ICU phoned me at home asking that Jonathan and I go into the hospital immediately as Sheila had deteriorated suddenly and markedly. As Jonathan drove us through the empty streets, we prayed desperate prayers like those of drowning men. My mind was leaping wildly from Sheila's present condition to making arrangements for her funeral.

On our arrival at ICU, the doctor told us there was little hope. We waited, watching and praying throughout the night. Yet, once again, Sheila did not die. She clung to life as if by her fingernails. By 8.30 am, Jonathan and I were on our way home, exhausted, unable to stay awake any longer.

During extended prayer times each evening after I came home from ICU around 10 pm, I prayed through Psalm 118. Why Psalm 118? Well, prior to her hospitalisation, Sheila and I had been reading through the Psalms. Psalm 118 was the last one we had read together. This was where we were when she became ill. It became the basis of my prayers for Sheila, and I noted verses 17 and 18: 'I will not die but live, and will proclaim what the Lord has done. The Lord has chastened me severely but he has not given me over to death.'

Three Christian friends who were widely separated geographically, in Ireland, Singapore and Jakarta, all contacted me independently and gave me exactly the same verses – Psalm 27:13 and 14 – 'I am still confident of this: I will see the goodness of the Lord in the land of the living. Wait for the Lord; be strong and take heart and wait for the Lord.' Through these assurances I was becoming confident that, in spite of recent deterioration and a poor prognosis, Sheila would be healed in answer to prayer.

I asked the Lord one evening to confirm the line of prayer that I was taking for Sheila's recovery, if it was coming from him, through prompting someone else to bring me the same message. The next morning, a former OMF colleague, the Rev. Howard Peskett, phoned me. After enquiring about Sheila, he quoted Psalm 66 beginning with verse 8: 'Praise our God, O peoples, let the sound of his praise be heard; he has preserved our lives and kept our feet from slipping,' and ending, 'Praise be to God who has not rejected my prayer or withheld his love from me!' Then Howard prayed for Sheila's healing. I saw this as the

Lord's response to my evening prayer. I was over the moon – Sheila was going to recover! Only the Lord had known of my request. I thought of Psalm 118 and how it would be fulfilled, 'I will not die but live, and will proclaim what the Lord has done.'

When Jonathan and I went into ICU on Christmas Day, the Christian consultant on duty said, as he shook our hands, 'I can't wish you a *happy* Christmas but I can wish you a *joyous* one.' That day, drains were inserted in Sheila's chest and eventually four pints of fluid were removed. Her condition was still critical but plateaued as December crawled to its weary end for us.

The doctors felt she could still recover. Laboratory cultures had shown by then that the virus which had attacked Sheila was influenza type A and that it had immobilised her immune system. On 29th December, one consultant said, 'Influenza type A is frequently fatal when linked to pneumonia but Mrs Miller has survived it. Your wife will be on the ventilator till at least the end of next week – the best scenario – and in ICU for several more weeks. I feel it is best for your son to return to his work in Bangkok now.' I sensed this dedicated doctor was now more optimistic. In addition I also had the inner conviction that in spite of the great danger Sheila was still in, all would be well.

Jonathan and I were deeply impressed with the Belfast City Hospital. At every level – doctors, sisters, nurses, auxiliary staff, chaplain – we were shown the utmost consideration. Questions were fully answered, information was offered, compassion was combined with efficiency. Never had I experienced care like this, and having had ten operations including heart and kidney surgery, I'd had reasonably wide experience of hospitals at home and abroad. This was far in advance of anything I'd experienced before. Bedside visits by the Presbyterian chaplain, Muriel Cromie, were inspirational. I later found out that the hospital administrator was a keen Christian who regularly took time to visit patients. He had been to Sheila's bedside in my absence and prayed for her.

On 30th December, Jonathan paid his final visit to see Sheila. Then I drove him to Belfast's Aldergrove Airport. Life settled into a daily routine for me – an early morning phone call to ICU, a noon visit to the hospital until 4 pm, a meal at home or with friends, back to ICU from 7 until 9 pm, phone calls, prayer, Bible study, and bed at midnight.

I used the time waiting by Sheila's bedside to write to friends asking them to pray for Sheila. Letters and cards were pouring in. My fax was churning out long-distance messages of concern and support. My answer-phone was brimful of messages.

One card from a prayer partner quoted Psalm 119:116 – 'Sustain me according to your promise and I will live; do not let my hopes be dashed.' In contrast, some consultants were saying, 'No change is not a hopeful sign. The longer this goes on, doctors tend towards pessimism.'

ICU in Belfast City Hospital is an open ward. In the bed next to Sheila lay a woman who was, by then, very seriously ill. Her husband Harry and I had often chatted as we waited in the corridor while staff worked with our loved ones. That evening he came over to me as I sat at Sheila's bedside. Harry, quiet-spoken and gentle, was very worried. He felt his wife was dying.

'I don't know what to do,' he said. 'I feel I can't cope.'

'Would you like me to pray for her and you, Harry?' I asked.

'Yes, I would,' he replied and immediately squatted on the floor beside me. I committed them both into the Lord's care, asking for his help. A wonderful thing happened. After thanking me, Harry said, 'I feel completely different now. I feel I can cope. When this is all over, can I come and see you, John?' I assured him he could.

Two days later when I came into ICU, his wife was gone,

having died the previous evening. I wrote a letter of sympathy to Harry.

On 15th January, a week after I had prayed with Harry in ICU, I received a card from a friend in Milltown Baptist Church, Belfast. In it he referred to 2 Corinthians 1:3–5. I was reading the card in my study, so I reached to a bookshelf for a Bible to check the verses. I took down *The Message* – a paraphrase by Dr Eugene Peterson that Sheila and I had come to love. This is what I read: 'All praise to the God and Father of our Master, Jesus the Messiah! Father of all mercy! God of all healing counsel! He comes alongside us when we go through hard times, and before you know it, he brings us alongside someone else who is going through hard times so that we can be there for that person just as God was there for us.'

At that point the telephone rang. I had *The Message* open in my left hand and the phone in the other. It was Harry! I remember thinking, 'Harry is the one whom the Lord wants me to get alongside.' We each enquired how the other was doing and arranged to be in further contact.

Sheila's plateau continued. Pumactant, a drug used for the lung development of premature babies, was tried in the hope of buying time to enable the recovery of lung functions. Improvement occurred but was not sustained. On Wednesday 17th January 1996, Dr George said to me, 'Everything is decided up above – by God. It is not in our hands. We can only co-operate. The reduced swelling is a good sign. Recovery will be slow. I am more hopeful now than I was earlier. Mrs Miller's survival chance is still 50/50 but she is not going down.'

Physically, I was feeling exhausted but I was being strengthened by visits from Christian friends in OMF and from St Mary's, my home church in Dundonald. All during those weeks, the Rev. John Dixon, the OMF council chairman, asked me out to lunch on a weekly basis. His prayers were inspirational. He even came to pray on Christmas Day! Here was Emmanuel – God with us – on 25th December through his servant. John's visits over those weeks were invaluable, for in the midst of all his busyness he ministered to me in depth. The Rev. John White, my pastor, came frequently to pray with Sheila and me, sometimes accompanied by church leaders David and Tommy. Once they anointed Sheila with oil as we prayed. I sensed the privilege it was to belong to the family of God. These visits and those of other pastors communicated love and deep concern.

Sheila's plateau ended on Thursday 18th January, when she developed a chest infection. Doctors had warned that if this happened it could be fatal. I was, by now, writing frenetically for prayer cover. One afternoon the hospital postman said, 'You seem to write a lot of letters.'

I replied, 'Yes. My wife is critically ill. I'm writing to people asking them to pray for her.' I asked him if he was a Christian.

'Yes, I am,' he replied, and so are my two mates here. What is your wife's name?'

'Sheila Miller,' I replied.

'We'll pray for her,' he promised.

By Friday 19th January, Sheila had also taken a yeast infection. The duty consultant said, 'Things are very discouraging. They look very grim but we plod on. Her chest is actually improving but the two infections are now affecting her severely.' That was the most trying day I'd spent in ICU. At lunch-time on Saturday 20th January, Sheila was no worse but when I returned in the evening she was sinking fast. The new infection had taken over and was fast becoming irreversible. I knew this dreadful roller-coaster ride was nearly over. OMF's Irish director, Hugh, and I prayed outside while the staff worked with Sheila.

Dr McCarthy then told me Sheila would soon die. Was

there a friend I would like to call in? Would I like to phone my son in Bangkok? Jonathan asked me to say to Sheila, in case she might still be able to hear, that he could not have had a more beautiful mother in every respect. I repeated it to Sheila and through many tears committed her to the Lord with thanksgiving for giving me such a wonderful wife. My friend George Orr joined me at the bedside around 10 pm as Sheila was dying. I think Sheila went to be with the Lord around that time on Saturday 20th January, the day she was due to have spoken to Girl Crusaders leaders at a Day of Prayer. At 12.05 am the doctor said she was no longer with us but he was prepared to keep the life support machine on longer if I wished.

But we knew she was gone. The immensity of what had happened overwhelmed me as I phoned the news to Jonathan in Bangkok. George drove me to his home where Pat, Sheila's friend of more than fifty summers, wept with me as we met in their hall.

The following day, Sunday, was full of phone calls, visitors and making arrangements. The Christians were very supportive – OMFers, church leaders from St Mary's Ballybeen, relatives and the wider family of the Lord. I wondered how non-Christians coped at such times. I was finding bereavement so painful, even with all this support, even when I knew the Lord was with me and I had the hope of the resurrection.

I had known the present rector of Hillsborough Parish Church when he was a boy in my home church in Londonderry. Sheila had loved the setting of that church. Just a few months earlier, Sheila and I had taken my two sisters who were visiting us from Canada and England to see it. Little did we know that within a few months Sheila would be buried in its adjacent cemetery, for Canon John Dinnen was able to make a grave plot available. I knew Sheila would have approved. How gracious our God is even in the provision of a grave, but then, as Psalm 116:15 reminds us, 'Precious in the sight of the Lord is the death of his saints.'

Jonathan flew into Belfast's Aldergrove Airport clutching a huge box of Thai orchids. A local florist shaped them into wreaths from Jonathan, Cornelia and me. His card contained this inscription, 'For my beautiful Mum. How I love you; how I'll miss you – J-boy and Cornelia.'

That day was spent making arrangements for the funeral. Jonathan's background in journalism was so helpful at the printers. The registrar of deaths, like the printer, was a committed Christian. God's people were everywhere. We drove home to Saintfield where we made ready for friends who would call to sympathise. My neighbour Carol came in and acted as hostess. When Sheila and I had arrived in Saintfield in December 1994, Carol had offered her friendship from the start. I remember her saying to Sheila and me, 'I believe God has brought you both here for us.' Later I would better understand that statement.

Healing and comfort flowed as J-boy and I shared our feelings that evening. Day and night I could hardly stop crying. I recall saying to my friend George, 'I don't know how I'll ever cope with life again.' And I remember how compassionately, yet so confidently, he said, 'You *will* cope, John, and you will come through. God will see to that.' That answer has stayed with me – as has the attentive, concerned gaze which he fixed on me. He and Pat have been the major instruments the Lord has used to bring me through all the sorrow. Friendship like theirs is priceless.

I phoned my friend Harry whose wife had died two weeks earlier. He said he would like to come up from Newry for the service in church.

The day of Sheila's funeral, 24th January 1996, was bitterly cold but dry. The church was filled with friends and relatives. Seeing the faces of several OMF friends from

England was wonderfully encouraging. Then there was Ismet, son of Junaya, a Syrian friend with whom Sheila had studied the Bible in our home in Singapore. He had flown over from London for the funeral. Sheila had invested much time in that relationship with Junaya and her daughter Angelika. I wonder if Sheila knew that Ismet had come to the church and graveside? It would have thrilled her.

God had arranged that the OMF General Director, David Pickard, with whom Sheila and I had worked for over a decade, was in Britain at that very time. Imagine the Lord arranging for David to be here for Sheila's funeral! That was very special to me and the message from his heart ministered God's grace to many.

The prayer time led by the Rev. John Dixon brought a profound sense of the Lord's presence as several friends of Sheila thanked God for her life and ministry. We sang her favourite hymns, and Ruth, our church organist, did what Sheila loved as we sang the closing verse of 'There is a redeemer' – she moved up a key. Many people sensed the glory of God and the joy of heaven.

The graveside service in the historic cemetery was short. The sense of the enemy-ness of death in depriving us of our loved one was profound as the orchids and daffodils were placed on the grave. Jonathan and I stood, arms on each other's shoulders. 'Pray now, Dad,' he urged as we gazed on those flowers and through our tears thanked our loving heavenly Father for giving us such a radiant woman as wife and mother.

Numbness, unreality, disbelief that Sheila had died – these words best describe how I felt then and in the succeeding weeks; also the searing inner pain, the sense of loss – which hurt more than the angina before my heart surgery.

With Jonathan only able to stay a few more days, I needed to take some decisions. A month before her illness,

Sheila and I took advantage of a free offer from Marks and Spencer to have our portraits taken. Two days after the funeral Jonathan and I went to the photographers in Lisbon for a slide presentation. Sheila looked so healthy and beautiful on the screen. She had always been very photogenic. 'How could someone looking like that have died so soon afterwards?' I asked myself in the silence. I was thrilled to have such recent photographs available even though the selection procedure was in such distressing circumstances.

My friend George knew that I also wanted to arrange for a memorial stone for Sheila's grave while J-boy was still with me. He made an appointment for us and we went to this after seeing the photographer. I wanted Jonathan to help me with the choice of stone and with the wording of the inscription. The owner of the firm was away on business but his son gave us the information we needed competently and sensitively. He advised as J-boy and I wrote the words down:

MILLER

WITH THANKS TO THE LORD FOR

SHEILA PATRICIA

18TH SEPTEMBER, 1934 – 21ST JANUARY, 1996

SHE LOVED THE GOD WHO GAVE HER RAINBOWS

RADIANT WIFE OF JOHN AND MOTHER OF JONATHAN

HE SET ETERNITY IN HER HEART – ECCLESIASTES 3:11

OMF CHEFOO SCHOOL MALAYSIA, SINGAPORE AND SAINTFIELD

We chose granite from the nearby Mountains of Mourne. It was more expensive but beautiful. When we had settled on the wording, and the young man was assured that we were certain of our choice, he said, 'I hope you do not mind my mentioning this, but my father would like to provide this memorial stone without charge. He is interested in Christian missionary work and would like to provide this for you. You see, my mother was part of a prayer circle that had been praying for your wife.' I struggled with my surging emotions as I experienced yet again the faithfulness and generous provision of our loving heavenly Father.

When Sheila and I had set out as missionaries nearly twenty-six years earlier, we had been aware of the Lord's promise in Mark 10:29–30 – '"I tell you the truth," Jesus replied, "no one who has left home or brothers or sisters or mother or father or children or fields for me and the gospel will fail to receive a hundred times as much in this present age (homes, brothers, sisters, mothers, children and fields – and with them persecutions) and in the age to come, eternal life."' The Lord had been faithful to his promises all through the years of Sheila's life. Now here, at the end of her life, he was still providing that hundredfold.

When a Christian dies in Malaysia and Singapore, friends bring monetary gifts to help with the funeral expenses. When Sheila died, several gifts from our Asian Christian friends arrived within a few days. These fully covered every expense and I marvelled again at God's faithfulness. In addition, over £4,000, given in memory of Sheila, was forwarded to the two major ministries that Sheila loved and in which she had invested her life – OMF and Jewish people.

Two Christian medical friends, Professor Brew Atkinson and Dr Grace Pettigrew, gave me wise counsel in the weeks after my bereavement. They explained to me that grieving is hard work and I would feel very tired. They advised me not to allow myself to be closed in. I made sure I went to church twice each Sunday and attended our stimulating cell group mid-week. I spent one evening a week with Pat and George. George and I played a couple of hours of snooker in the evening. I began flute lessons for the first time in March and started preaching in April. The latter was difficult at first but I am glad now that I started at that time.

The relationship between Sheila and her mother had been very close. Now Mum was in great distress. Her remaining daughter was dead and her eighty-eight-year-old husband was in hospital, permanently. J-boy and I drove to Londonderry before he left Ireland to be with them. On the way home we visited Limavady Baptist Church, for Pastor Smyth, his wife and the members had been very supportive. I was still in shock but I vividly recall one sentence which has lingered in my mind since that evening. A group of us had been discussing the 'why?' of Sheila's death in the pastor's home. Quietly Pastor Smyth said, 'I just believe it was God's time for Sheila to go to him.' Doubts about medical care for Sheila in the first small local hospital, and related issues of second causes, were settled for me then, though I suspect the pastor did not realise the comfort I drew from his words 'I just believe it was God's time'.

The next day, J-boy left for Bangkok, where he was soon immersed in the hectic life of a BBC World Service correspondent. A fax from a former OMF colleague from New Zealand had advised, 'Don't miss the lessons.' That had stuck in both our minds. Before he flew off, J-boy highlighted one of the main ones we had both learnt: 'Mum stuck with people, even difficult people. She never wrote anyone off. When I see what those people thought of Mum, I realise I must not write people off either.'

Some months before Sheila became ill, I had told her that I had noticed how the relationships she formed were much deeper than mine. As letters and cards arrived by their hundreds from all over the world, I discovered that my statement was far truer than I had ever realised. I resolved to build on her relationships in the months and years ahead. First, I decided to reply personally to every letter, not only with the letter that I had had printed but also by enclosing a hand-written one or by adding a footnote. This took months to do but the Lord used it as a ministry in both directions – to others and to me. Sheila's first Jewish friend in Singapore had written, 'Now I have no link to God any more. Sheila was my link to him, I felt. Thank you for telling me that Sheila prayed for me till the end. I never knew that.' Letters sharing deep sentiments came in day after day. I read them and wept as I began to understand a little of what God had been doing through Sheila's relationships over the years.

Secondly, I asked my team of forty prayer partners to pray that Sheila 'though dead' would still 'speak' through her books. Over the next months I was to learn of several answers to that prayer, one occurring before the prayer had even been formed.

I was speaking in Londonderry in October 1996 on the verse, 'I tell you the truth, unless a kernel of wheat falls to the ground and dies, it remains only a single seed. But if it dies, it produces many seeds' (John 12:24). Afterwards a woman came up to me and said she had an illustration of the verse. Maud told me that she managed the Red Cross Charity shop in the Diamond in Londonderry. She had read Sheila's autobiography *I Can Trace A Rainbow* and spoken to her about it; she also had a copy of the book in her shop. One day in December 1995, a woman came into the shop and Maud indicated Sheila's book and said to her, 'You need to read this. It could help you. The person who wrote it is seriously ill in hospital just now.' Thus urged, the customer bought the book. Three weeks later she returned to say, 'Do you remember advising me to buy and read a certain book? Well, I did read it and my life will never be the same again.' Listening to Maud's story, I was moved to think that the Lord had been using Sheila's writing even while she had been unconscious and on life support at Belfast's ICU.

That autumn, I was giving the Bible messages at a conference in London for those who produce Christian films in Europe. A Dutch production had won the competition for the best film. Two days later at dinner I was sitting opposite Yenny Nabers who had won the top award. I congratulated her. One of her media colleagues urged her to tell me about her next project. She did so very reluctantly: 'It's a film for children and is the story of a missionary who faced a major problem. He prayed. God answered his prayer by sending an elephant!' I asked if I might tell Yenny a story. She nodded.

'Yenny, the person who wrote the story you are making the film about was my wife, Sheila.' In utter amazement Yenny took a copy of Sheila's book *Ian and the Gigantic Leafy Obstacle* from her bag. The tape in my mind went into rewind as I recalled the prayer request that the Lord would go on using Sheila's books. I had never imagined this answer.

My friendship with Harry continues. Some weeks after Sheila's funeral, Harry came to my home for lunch. We talked at length about our loved ones, of heaven and of our bereavement. We prayed together. Months later when I began an Alpha group, Harry drove the thirty miles from Newry on Wednesdays to attend. Our friendship deepened. In December 1996 he phoned me and said, 'John, I often lie awake at night and think about my wife's death. I've come to the conclusion that God allowed her to die to bring me back to himself. It all began that night in ICU when we prayed together.'

Carol, my friendly neighbour, had said she believed God had brought Sheila and me to Saintfield for her, but now I was the one who was benefiting from her loving kindness. One day she said to me, 'John, whenever I talked to Sheila she always ended our conversation with the words, "God bless you, Carol." Would you be prepared to do the same?' I agreed and if I forgot, Carol would say with a smile, 'John, you've forgotten!' Then I began to make this my prayer for Carol – that God would bless her. And he did! Yet Carol became ill and had to be admitted to the same hospital as Sheila had died in. The night before her admission, Carol came over to ask me to pray for her in her distress. I did and we talked about committing ourselves to the Lord. Carol said she had already done that, so we thanked him for coming into her life after looking at Revelation 3:20 together. The Lord helped Carol through her time in hospital. She came to the Alpha group too, and after the first study said, 'I have a new vision of Jesus.' Later she phoned me to say, 'I'm sitting at home and I am filled with joy to think that the Holy Spirit is living in me. The hymns in church have new meaning for me now.'

That Alpha group brought me tremendous joy too. Almost everyone attending was there because of Sheila. One day, Mabel, who had been Sheila's teacher in a cross-stitch class, said, 'Just think, John, all of this Alpha group happened because of Sheila.' Recently I discovered that, early in my bereavement, Lorna, one of my prayer partners, had asked the Lord to give me a ministry that would bring me great joy to replace all the sorrow. How fully he answered that request, giving me 'beauty for ashes, the oil of joy for mourning, the garment of praise for the spirit of heaviness' (Isaiah 61:3).

Since Sheila's death I have thought much about prayer, for I had been so sure that the Lord was going to restore Sheila in response to believing prayer.

'So do you feel God let you down, John?' my friend Howard asked me.

'No,' I replied, 'but I don't understand.' That was 23rd January 1996.

Over the first year of bereavement, the Lord has given me fresh insights into prayer. He has reminded me that he is the one in control – that I cannot force him to act in the way I want, even in a life-or-death situation. I had almost come to the point where I felt he *must* answer because of the volume and urgency of our prayers. The hardest prayer

I ever prayed was the one I came to one evening, alone, 'Father, if you are willing, heal Sheila; yet not my will, but yours be done.' At first I could barely trust him to take control in case he decided to take Sheila to heaven. So praying that prayer was a major step for me. When I prayed it, I heaved a huge sigh of relief – the burden was off my shoulders. An accountant friend had once told me he felt our professional training often influences how we approach life. 'As an accountant, I've been trained to suspect people – to try and find out who has been fiddling the books. As a consequence, I am suspicious of people's motives in life,' he said. I had applied that principle to myself as a trained teacher, and felt that it spoke into the area of teaching and communications – make your message simple, digestible. However, one evening a church friend said, 'As a teacher, I'm in control of the situation in a classroom.' That was it! Through prayer, I, the teacher, was trying to put myself in the driving seat to take God where I wanted him. Accessibility to God through prayer did not give me control over him. I had known this as theological truth but there was a gap between my theology and my practice of prayer.

In November 1996, a letter from Esther began God's highlighting of another facet of prayer. As a girl, Esther had been in Sheila's Sunday school class. Now she was a primary school teacher herself. Her class had visited the residential home in which Sheila's mother lived. Esther read her pupils one of Sheila's books as a serial story. The children decided to write to Mrs Rankin to tell her how they were enjoying it. One eleven-year-old girl wrote, 'I am really enjoying your daughter's story *I Went to School in the Jungle*. . . . If I were you I would be very sad and angry after all you have been through with Sheila dying when she came home.'

But Mrs Rankin died suddenly on the very day Esther was posting the letters, so she sent them to me instead. She asked me to read them and write a reply to the children. Could I go to the school and speak to the children? Of course I could. I wanted to respond to that little girl's thoughtful comment about anger. I found that simplifying what I felt about Sheila's death for the children's understanding helped to crystallise my own thoughts: 'Mrs Rankin and I both felt very sad for we missed Sheila terribly. But we were not angry with God because we know what he is like. He's very loving and very good. So we can trust him even when we do not understand why, for we know he would never allow anything to happen that would do us any harm.'

Interestingly, far from being discouraged by my experiences of prayer, I've recently been entering into new dimensions in prayer. Never before have I been so aware of God's goodness and faithfulness. Each morning I look forward with excitement to my daily prayer times. In the month Sheila died, Monica, one of my former OMF co-workers in Singapore, wrote, 'And all those texts about life and living. Dear John, it seemed to me as I looked them up this morning . . . that these verses were for *you*. May they revive your heart again.' And in spite of the continuing feelings of loss and loneliness, the Lord has most certainly revived my heart again.

Sheila loved poetry. That is partly why I started this story with a poem. She began every chapter of her autobiography with one. It is fitting that this chapter should end similarly. This poem was written by Sheila's friend, Howard Peskett, on the evening of her funeral in which Howard had participated. He wrote it for Jonathan and me, and the Lord used it right from my first reading of it on 26th January 1996. I read it aloud to J-boy through my tears that Friday morning before we set out to order those photographs and the memorial stone. I can still clearly recall how the Holy Spirit ministered to us that day through Howard's inspired words:

With Him
(In memory of a lovely friend)

She is not here.
No more fingernail climbs back up cliffs of fall,
No more laboured gasps for breath,
    tangled in technological wizardry,
No more lilting welcome, sweet or grave,
No more lingering gaze, attentive to another's need,
No more lurking playfully behind the printed page,
    ready to jump out of words and scenes carefully crafted;
No – they are her epitaph. Her writings have squiggled to a
    stop.
Oh – Sheila!
No more, no where to be seen, in this life, again.
She has died. She is dead.
She is not here.

She is not there.
The school in the jungle, festooned with children,
An immaculate bungalow, fire warmly burning,
The flat in Cluny Road, where Jewish women gathered,
    where husbanded strength was poured out patiently,
Gone from Saintfield, from a new home,
    too shortly savoured.
Not in the box, adorned with orchids,
    and their remembrancers, 'Oh how I loved you!'
Not in the grave, interred under a winter sky:
A woman of God's image, life-full of joy,
    extinguished, life's whole sap sunk, into the ground.
She is not there.

She is not here.
She is not there.
She is WITH HIM,
This is the Christian faith:
Not like a tidelet sucked into an ocean,
Not fallen into a fathomless, unmentionable hole;
But gone to that land where all bright spirits dwell,

Praising for ever Him who made all times, and this;
Knowing, even as we utter these dull words,
   short-changed by time and space,
That the full reality, the weight of glory,
   as far exceeds them,
As golden fields of grain exhaust in glad surprise
The upward efforts of the buried seed.

Lift up your heads!
Call not back her who, Lent for ever over,
Rejoices in Easter-land with Him who triumphs,
   and with those who feast.
Yes, two words to dry (not stop) our tears:
She, Sheila, is . . .
WITH HIM.

Bibliography

Bibliography

Books on bereavement or other kinds of suffering

Alexander, Helen, *Bereavement – A Shared Experience* (Lion: Oxford)

Dunn, Ronald, *When Heaven Is Silent* (Word: Milton Keynes)

Hartill, Rosemary, *Were You There? Surviving Life's Setbacks*, based on the BBC Radio 4 series (SPCK: London)

Kushner, Harold, *When Bad Things Happen to Good People* (Pan Books: London)

Lewis, C. S., *A Grief Observed* (Faber: London)

Mitsch and Brookside, *Grieving the Loss of Someone You Love* (Hodder and Stoughton: London)

Shaw, Luci, *God in the Dark* (Highland: Crowborough)

Sittser, Gerald, *A Grace Disguised* (Hodder and Stoughton: London)

Yancey, Philip, *Disappointment with God* (Harper Collins: London)

Anthologies

Croucher, Rowland, *Gentle Darkness* (Lion: Oxford)

Whittaker, Agnes, *All in the End Is Harvest*, an anthology for those who grieve (DLT/Cruse: London)

Books of readings, comments and meditations or prayers

Askew, Eddie, *Cross Purposes* (Leprosy Mission International: Middlesex)
Askew, Eddie, *Facing the Storm* (Leprosy Mission International: Middlesex)

Precious to God
Sarah Bowen   £5.99 in UK

Two young people, delighted to be starting a family, have their expectations shattered by the arrival of a handicapped child. And yet this is only the first of many difficulties to be faced. What was initially a tragedy, is through faith, transformed into a story of inspiration, hope and spiritual enrichment.

'I was deeply moved by Sarah's story. Do read it.'
Celia Bowring

Angels Keep Watch
Carol Hathorne   £5.99 in UK

A true adventure showing how God still directs our lives, not with wind, earthquake or fire, but by the still small voice.

'Go to Africa.' The Lord had been saying it for over forty years. At last, Carol Hathorne had obeyed, going out to Kenya with her husband. On the eastern side of Nairobi, where tourists never go, they came face to face with dangers, hardship and poverty on a daily basis, but experienced the joy of learning that Christianity is still growing in God's world.

Carol Hathorne is an Anglican priest working in a parish near Dudley, West Midlands. Her husband, Mark, is a Methodist minister in the same area.

God's Catalyst
Rosemary Green   £8.99 in UK

The highly commended guide to prayer counselling.

Rosemary Green's international counselling ministry has prayer and listening to God at it's heart. Changed lives and rekindled faith testify to God's healing power. Here she provides insight, inspiration and advice for both counsellors and concerned lay Christians who long to be channels of God's Spirit to help those in need.

God's Catalyst is a unique tool for the non-specialist counsellor; for the pastor who has no training; for the lay Christian who wants to come alongside hurting friends.

'To read this book will be helpful to any Christian interested in helping others.'

John White

Women Celebrating Faith
Lucinda S. McDowell   £5.99 in UK

In this challenging and gripping collection, women from all walks of life take time to look back on their lives at forty and reflect on the spiritual lessons they've learned. No matter what your age you will be encouraged by the experiences of these women.

'A book that makes you look forward to mid-life.'

Susan Yates